Henry Nicholas Jarchow

Forest Planting

a treatise on the care of timber lands and the restoration of denuded wood-lands

on plains and mountains

Henry Nicholas Jarchow

Forest Planting
a treatise on the care of timber lands and the restoration of denuded wood-lands on plains and mountains

ISBN/EAN: 9783337287504

Printed in Europe, USA, Canada, Australia, Japan

Cover: Foto ©Andreas Hilbeck / pixelio.de

More available books at **www.hansebooks.com**

PREFACE.

THE act of the New York State Legislature, passed on the 15th day of May, 1885—which may justly be considered as inaugurating a new era in the forestry matters of the Empire State—directs the members of the Forest Commission "to prepare tracts or circulars "of information, giving plain and concise advice for "the care of wood-lands upon private lands, and for "the starting of new plantations upon lands that "have been denuded, exhausted by cultivation, eroded "by torrents, or injured by fire, or that are sandy, "marshy, broken, sterile, or waste and unfit for other "use." This well-meant instruction has not, to my knowledge, been carried into execution, very likely because we have no literature of any importance upon this subject—for forestry with us has not been regarded as being a branch of rural economy worthy of literary treatment, and, therefore, this field of culture has been left nearly untouched.

In this limited work I have attempted to bring within as small a compass as is consistent with clearness of statement the salient points of systematic forestry and its application to the restocking of denuded wood-lands on plains and mountains. American writers on forestry have mostly confined themselves to the treatment of forest trees as single trees, and not as masses of trees raised for the purpose of producing crops of wood or timber. They thought that forestry was an art of tree planting, destined to create, by artificial sowing and planting, new forests; and that, as we are still in the possession of many and large natural forests, the creation of new forests was to us a foreign matter. This is entirely wrong, for if we really will *preserve* our natural or wild forests—and this is undoubtedly a much better and cheaper policy than to continue destroying them, and to later raise, at an enormous cost and loss of time, artificial forests—we have to care for our woods just as fully as the artificial forests in the European countries are treated; for in the preservation of forests it makes no difference at all whether they are originated by nature or by human art, because both are subject to the same dangers and injuries. Unless the natural forests are managed systematically, we cannot but expect that the reparation of damages done to a forest either by accidents or elementary forces, or by the natural course of tree life, will take as many centuries as it would require decades for this purpose, if we assist nature in its regenerating endeavors through the means suggested by scientific forestry.

The condition in which our forests are now, is not such as to warrant us in "pooh-poohing" the idea of looking for instruction in this matter to the European nations, and to only glance at their methods of treating forests, because we have a different form of government (see Report of the N. Y. Forest Commission, 1886, page 67), or because "the entire condition of things here differs so materially from that in the old world." (See Report of the Forest Commission, 1887, page 17.) Certainly there is a great difference between our government and that of most of the European nations, and politico-economical matters are often treated here differently from what they are there; but this does not affect the question of preserving to the succeeding generations the *natural resources* of a country necessary for the welfare of its inhabitants. If we cannot invent better methods of preserving forests than those we have practiced up to the present time, and by which our forests will soon be doomed to total extinction, we should not only glance at, but study European systems closely, and inquire into the possibility of adopting them to some extent, if necessary. If we do that we will find that, without "*making the elaborate science and intricate machinery of European forestry available in this State*" (see Second Annual Report of the Forest Commission, Albany, 1887, page 17), the preservation of our woods can be accomplished, and at the same time a continued and even enlarged exploitation may be secured by applying some similar methods, subject of course to such changes as are rendered necessary by a diversity of climate, soil and local influences.

Although twenty years' experience in forestry in northern Germany, combined with personal observation in this country, during a like period, would seem to justify me in urging the practicability of introducing systematic forestry into the United States, I do not intend to express here a positive opinion on this point. During the course of my experience in this State, I have heard and read so much regarding the necessity of arresting the reckless use and destruction of our forests, that I thought the time had at last arrived to answer the question, "*How shall we preserve our forests?*" with a practical work. In the following pages I have endeavored to furnish sufficient hints to those who are interested in this important matter, to form a correct opinion in regard to the requirements of the culture of forests, and to apply the acquired knowledge to the proper preservation of wild or natural forests, and the restoration of wood-lands which have been denuded.

In the arrangement of the chapters, I have been led by a desire to give not only reliable information upon the subject, but also to furnish teachers in forest culture a more practical guide than they have found hitherto in American books. No claim for completeness is made, the less so as it is only a pioneer destined to invite better and more experienced men to treat more fully upon a subject, the importance of which is more and more felt every year. The enumeration and description of our common forest trees has been omitted intentionally, as these topics are treated by others with great thoroughness.

The Diagrams given in Chapter IX, Part II, and in Chapter III, Part III, explain themselves, and show the engineering work to be done in covering downs on the sea-coast with trees, and in reforesting mountains when their slopes have been cleared of natural woods, and torrents with deep ravines have been formed. The views showing the gorgeous scenery of the Adirondacks are not, perhaps, necessary to the book; but they are given to arouse those who are unaware of the beauties of our native mountain forests, and to create a spirit of enthusiasm which shall not only help to prevent further devastation of our State forests, but also may assist in restocking the wantonly denuded wood-lands.

To a good agriculturist with sufficient experience in the nature and behavior of the principal forest trees, it will not be difficult to apply the given instructions so as to accomplish the principal objects of modern forestry in the preservation of wild or natural forests.

Although the present book is written only with regard to the requirements of the State of New York, there is no reason why the instructions given in its pages should not be applicable to other localities, where the same conditions exist, if the proper allowance is made for diversity of climate, soil and topography.

THE AUTHOR.

CONTENTS.

PART I.—Forest Culture.

PART II.—Forest Planting on Plains.

PART III.—Forest Planting on Mountains.

FOREST PLANTING.

PART I.—FOREST CULTURE.

CHAPTER I.

INTRODUCTORY REMARKS.

About sixty years ago, Governor DeWitt Clinton, in a message to the Legislature of New York, urged the fostering of forest planting, and declared that the reproduction of our woods was an object of primary importance. This sensible advice did not receive that legislative consideration which the great interests involved therein merited. The devastation of our forests, especially of those situated in the Adirondack region, went on as before, nay even increased from year to year, so that now the formerly densely wooded summits of those mountains are nearly denuded. We will not expatiate here on the calamities which have already befallen the country by the continual deforestation of our mountains, and which undoubtedly will in time grow to much larger dimensions; we only point to the fact that since the axe of the tanner, lumberman and miner has reached the previously well-stocked high plateaus on the Adirondacks (whence the sources of the Hudson, the Black River, some tributaries of the Mohawk and other rivers take their rise), our noble Hudson river has lost nearly five feet in its average depth. This fall in the level of the river will undoubtedly continue, unless an effective stop is put to the further deforestation of the Adirondacks, and the reforestation of the denuded wood-lands thereon is begun. But here we encounter difficulties which apparently are scarcely to be overcome. For it is not so much the inclemency of the climate, or the exposure of the location, or the poorness of the soil, which prevents the restoration of our mountain forests; it is the fact that of the four millions of acres covering the Adirondacks, only eight hundred thousand belong to the State, while the remaining three millions and two hundred thousand acres are the property of private owners—and these, in general, have neither the intention nor the desire to be troubled with forest planting. They strip off every valuable tree, and when their lands become unprofitable allow them to be sold for taxes. In this way a great many acres reverted to the original owner, the State, as nobody found it desirable to buy denuded or devastated wood-lands.

In 1872 the "Park Commissioners," it is true, recommended that in the mountainous regions of our State no more State lands should be sold, and that, as lands reverted from non-payment of taxes, they be held for future *forest management.* This advice, however, was not acted upon until 1885, when the State, notwithstanding the sales that had been effected during the interval, had again become the owner of about eight hundred thousand acres of wood-lands.

To the Legislature of 1885 is due a new and sound departure in the forestry interests of our State; for by the act passed on the 15th day of May, 1885, a Forest Commission was established, whose duty it was to preserve the State forests, and the former recommendation of the "Park Commissioners" was made obligatory. At present none of the State lands situate in the counties embracing the Adirondack and Catskill mountains can be sold or leased; but every piece of land situated in those counties which may in the future be acquired by the State, shall be added to the State lands and forever *kept as a forest preserve.*

From the first annual report of the State Forest Commission, published at Albany in 1886, it appears that the gentlemen forming that Commission had at that time a correct view in regard to the extent of their duties, for on page 12 they declare that they not only must protect the preserve against ravages by the elements (fire), and against the army of thieves and trespassers who are plundering the State forests, but that there should be devised a system "*which would, in time, make these forests not only self-sustaining as to cost of management, but, in addition, a source of wealth and revenue to the commonwealth.*"

With these words the Commissioners expressed an idea the proper consideration of which would ensure the introduction of systematic forest culture. For it was not so much the decreasing area of woods, nor the increasing demand for forest products, which led in the European territories to the introduction of the present so highly esteemed forest culture; it was the necessity of deriving the highest possible permanent revenue from the forests. And this dire necessity performed what for want of means and knowledge could not be done in former times. But as soon as the owners of large forests, especially the corporations, possessors of entailments, and governments in Europe, were forced to look upon the forests as a *perpetual source of revenue,* there were found the means and the knowledge of scientific or systematic management of forests.

In order to avoid any misconception in regard to the words "scientific forestry," it may here be observed that this expression does not designate any exact science; but just such management of forests, the practical results of which had been retraced to their scientific basis, and were found to be in harmony with scientific principles. For this reason the advanced forest economy of to-day is called scientific or systematic forestry, and this means: First, *to continually have a sustained forestal production from a certain area;* Second, *the natural regeneration of the forests;* and, Third, *a progressive improvement of the forests, instead of former deterioration.*

That the introduction of systematic forestry into our State forests would lead to a revenue for the State there can be no doubt, provided the management should be entrusted to experts. But at present we must drop this question entirely, as we have to concentrate every effort to the restocking of the many denuded public wood-lands in the State, and to inducing owners of the adjoining private woods to enter into a combination among themselves and with the public officers, in order to protect their wood-lands against damages, and to improve them by adopting the same measures which ought to be maintained in the State preserve. For it is a great drawback to the effective management of our State forests that they are not compact bodies of larger extent, but mostly disconnected plots, situated in different counties, ranging from a few acres up to many thousands, and usually surrounded by private lands, and, therefore, inaccessible by roads. As systematic forestry cannot be advantageously applied except on larger areas of compact bodies of wood-lands, it is evident that means must be devised to urge upon the adjoining owners of those private wood-lands, the necessity of entering into a combination with the managers of the State forests, and of a preconcerted action with them in regard to the preservation of their forests. There is no doubt that in the future such a combination will be agreed to, but not until the managers of the State forests upon the larger tracts have shown that a systematic forest economy is more profitable than the reckless felling of trees now going on in the private forests.

It might be advisable for the State to buy up small plots in limited numbers for the purpose of rounding off the boundaries of one or the other of the larger wood tracts owned by the State. But to obtain control over all the Adirondack forests by a general purchase—as is recommended by some—would be for many reasons very objectionable. Owners of those forests in the Adirondacks which are necessary for securing a continual flow of water to the rivers and streams could—as we will see in Chapter IV—be compelled by legislative measures to manage their woods so as to keep the grounds covered and protected against the influence of sun and air; and this is the only object it is desirable for the State to control the management of private forests of that character. But even if this question was, from the standpoint of the "right of eminent domain," decided in favor of the State, our government would not be able to undertake the exercise of this privilege unless there were secured for the service of the State men who understand how to systematically manage those mountain forests, which are called *protective* forests.

If we want to do our full duty toward those who are to come after us in this richly endowed country, we must repair, before it is too late, the damages done to the mountain forests in our State by the avarice and ignorance of the last two generations; and if the Forest Commission adhere to their programme, outlined in the cited first annual report, we will succeed in the restoration of the old, splendid wild forests of the Adirondacks. For properly *preserved* forests have :

(1) To be guarded by officers from the encroachment of persons who have no right in them, and from abuses and infractions of the law by those who have.

(2) To be protected from injury of various kinds, as for instance, from fires or other elementary damage, from destruction caused by pasturing farm animals or game, and from injuries caused by insects.

(3) In a properly conducted forest preserve there must be performed the following principal labors:

(*a*) Annual felling of mature, defective or dead trees, and their transportation in such a way that no damage shall be done to young growing trees.

(*b*) The periodical thinning out of places where the trees have sprung up too thickly, in order to effect a more vigorous growth to the remaining trees. At the same time the worthless kinds of trees are cleared out to give room for the more valuable.

(*c*) Vacant spots have to be filled out by *natural reproduction* of the trees, either by shoots, sprouts and layers from the stumps and roots, or by the natural sowing of the seed of the parent trees; or, finally, if in the way mentioned a reproduction of the trees is not practicable, *artificial* replanting, such as sowing the seed or planting young trees raised in forest nurseries, has to be resorted to, although this should be done as rarely as possible.

From the foregoing we perceive that the duties of the authorities in charge of our State forest preserve do not end when the grown up or planted trees have been cared for and protected to their full growth, but when they have been cut down and others started in their places.

If our forest preserve were conducted in some such way we should not any longer be compelled to witness every year the dying away of the enormous masses of trees and going to rot, killing young saplings and preventing others from springing up; besides furnishing the materials for originating and maintaining destructive forest fires. These dead trees are the headquarters for breeding beetles, bugs and other insects which prey upon the sound trees and destroy them long before they have reached their maturity.

Under all circumstances steps should at once be taken to establish on a proper place in the Adirondacks a *nursery* for raising the principal common forest trees, to be used upon the denuded State lands. This institution could later on be enlarged and also serve both the purposes of an experimental station for forest trees and a forest school for training and educating good foresters. The best crude material for this class of men our Forest Commissioners will undoubtedly find among the inhabitants of the Adirondacks, and if they will give those men an opportunity to become conversant with the practical instructions approved by systematic forestry, they will no longer ridicule the possibility of finding scientific foresters among the denizens of the North Woods. (See Second Annual Report of the Forest Commission, Albany, 1887.)

CHAPTER II.

IMPORTANCE OF FOREST CULTURE.

THERE are over six million acres of wood-lands in the twenty-six million acres of land in our State. The great interests involved in such a vast area should in themselves lead to a close study of everything pertaining to the nature of forests, and their influence upon the welfare of our commonwealth. Moreover, the State being an owner of about 800,000 acres of those wood-lands,* the revenues of which would amount to a considerable sum, if the forests were properly managed, and every tax-payer should look into the matter and endeavor to help in introducing a system by which the State forests could be made profitable. Up to the present time they have not yielded any income to the State, but are considered by the people living in their neighborhood as a piece of "Commons," from which they have a right to cut down, and take away what pleases them. It was a good step in the right direction when the Forest Commissioners hunted down the thieves and endeavored to put a stop to that disgraceful traffic.†

Another reason why we should pay more heed to the forest matters of the State arises from the circumstance that agriculture and industry are daily increasing their demands for certain kinds of wood, and that there is no likelihood of obtaining any material which could be entirely substituted for these woods, as is the case with coal and iron, which have encroached for some time upon the old privileges of certain kinds of trees used formerly exclusively for fuel and timber. True, for a certain period we can, after the exhaustion of our own resources, import lumber and timber from other states, especially from Canada. But, as the same mania of destroying the forests from which our own State up to a recent date has suffered, is raging in that country, we cannot for any considerable length of time rely upon importations,

---

* The State forests are situated in the Adirondack wilderness, excepting about 50,000 acres in the Catskill region, most of which are in Ulster Co.

† It is a sad but true observation that the moral views of our people in regard to public property have a much lower standard than is entertained in the transaction of private business. This deplorable neglect of the duties owed to public affairs on the part of the people can only be remedied by giving to them the same supervision as to private affairs.

and, therefore, we should prepare to satisfy as far as possible the demands of our people by home production. It is very fortunate that coal and iron now cover many demands, which otherwise would have to be satisfied by still more recklessly cutting down our forests. And it is very favorable to our growing industries that we can, at present, easily import from other States nearly any kind of wood now in use. However, we should not trifle with the time that is thus left to us for considering and changing the modes of the present treatment of forests; but utilize it for the introduction of systematic forest culture, although *the benefits of which will not be fully enjoyed save by future generations.*

The present indications are that in the further development of our State the demand for those kinds of wood which are especially used in our industries, will be always on the increase. And, therefore, these indications must guide us in many other questions which will arise, when it is to be determined what kind of forest trees to grow in the various localities. We may follow this guidance the more safely, as with the decreasing stock of wood for industrial purposes, there will be undoubtedly a corresponding increase in its price, and, therefore, presumably the net revenue from systematically managed forests will in the future be much larger than we are at present able to imagine.

As to the revenue derived from well managed state forests, the official reports published yearly by the various German governments are very instructive. They give not only full information in regard to the average production of wood and the income from the forests, but also explain the particulars of the management by which their success has been attained. These publications have greatly encouraged the introduction of scientific forest culture in wood-lands belonging *both to corporations and private persons in Germany.* From one of the last publications, we see that the yearly average increase in wood to the acre was:

	Lumber and Timber.	Smaller Wood.
In Prussia	0.84 cubic yard.	1.04 cubic yard.
" Bavaria	1.34 "	1.60 "
" Elsace-Lothringen	1.20 "	1.68 "
" Baden	1.24 "	1.80 "
" Hesse	1.60 "	2.06 "
" Saxony	1.78 "	2.16 "
" Wurtemberg	1.86 "	2.22 "

The yearly average income was to the acre:

	Gross Amount.	Net Income.
In Prussia	$1.60	$0.70
" Bavaria	2.90	1.22
" Hesse	4.02	2.65
" Baden	4.60	3.68
" Wurtemberg	4.65	2.79
" Elsace-Lothringen	4.75	2.69
" Saxony	4.85	3.50

As to the condition and productiveness of forests, much certainly depends upon soil and climate, and, therefore, the southern German states with their more congenial climate and soil are expected to yield a larger crop of forestry products, and consequently greater revenues than the northern states. But the marked difference in the proceeds of the named states is caused by the fact that scientific forest culture was introduced in the southern German states much earlier than in the northern. The treatment of the forests in the Kingdom of Saxony is conceded to be superior to any other, and, therefore, the output and net increase there is the largest.

To the private owner the revenues from forests are of course still larger, he being able to make of every forestry product a much more profitable use than the state, while the expenses of a private management are far below those of the government or corporations.

Under these circumstances, it is no wonder that forest culture on the eastern hemisphere of our globe is making great advances. For centuries there progressive science advocated only one side of field culture, viz., the agriculture; but now it is also vindicating the natural rights of the other side, viz., the forest culture. The combination of these ideas is expressed by the principle that wherever agriculture does not prove remunerative, while the cultivation of forests would indicate material profits, there is the proper place for sylviculture.

Finally, it may not be amiss to call attention to the fact that fine forests, besides giving inexpressible charms and attractions to the country, and thereby exercising a refining influence upon the moral and æsthetical sentiments of the people in general, serve as a resort for invalids, owing to the air which imparts vigor to the recuperative powers of those who are weak of nerve and broken in health. This is especially applicable to the Adirondack and Catskill mountain forests, whither every year hundreds of thousands of those who have lost their energy in the daily battle of city life flee to seek restoration by inhaling the invigorating mountain air, and enjoying out-of-door life.

CHAPTER III.

PROPORTION OF THE WOOD-LANDS TO THE TOTAL AREA OF A COUNTRY.

The influence of forests upon the climate of a country is undoubtedly important, and it cannot be denied that forests exercise also a marked effect upon the aqueous conditions of a certain territory. But, as far as experience in this State goes, the devastation of the forests on the plains has not essentially diminished the annual *quantity* of rain, although the general decreasing depth of the Hudson River convincingly tells of the losses caused by devastating the head waters of that stream at the summits and slopes of the Adirondacks. The destructive methods of forest exploitation with us are felt by the increasing abrupt changes of cold and heat, and of dry and wet spells. Forests retain much longer the humidity received in the shape of rain, snow, dew, etc, than the open fields, and they, therefore, promote the frequency of showers when a current of moist air strikes them. Owing to this peculiarity we justly consider the forests as equalizers in the distribution of rainfall during the seasons, and, as the fury of the violent winds which cause the abrupt changes of temperature can only be broken by a mass of elastic trees, we cannot deny that woods located either on the plains or mountains are the only means to mitigate the sudden changes from heat to cold.*

But the most beneficial influence is exercised by the forests to the neighboring territory, as their capability of receiving great quantities of moisture, and retaining them by protecting the soil against swift evaporation, renders them the most reliable reservoirs for the water in the subsoil, an element of the greatest importance for a successful pursuit of agriculture. It is a fact that wherever large tracts of woods have been cut down, the level of the ground water has been lowered sometimes to ten inches and more, and by that the cultivation of many plants which formerly thrived in such places has been made impossible. Clover, for instance, was raised in ancient times in Greece. After the country became denuded of forests, the culture of clover, requiring a moist atmosphere, had to be abandoned, and passed from

* Unfortunately our principal mountains extend from north to south. If they ran from east to west, we should have a climate such as Italy enjoys, as the most troublesome winds come to us from the northwest, against which the present formation of our mountains offers no protection.

there to Italy. But the devastation of the forests during the period of the "migration of the nations" caused such droughts that the culture of clover had to be given up in Italy, and it found a new start in southern Germany. Here clover has been cultivated for centuries with the most pronounced success. But during the last century the wooded area has been much encroached upon, and since that time clover culture began to decrease there, and to move into the moister climate of north Germany.

The consideration of the importance of the woods for a country has led to the question as to the proportion the wooded area of a country should bear to the whole territory, in order to secure the full benefit of the forests for the state. The economists generally contend that for this purpose twenty to twenty-five per cent of the total territory should be kept in wood. If this be true, our Empire State would come up fully to this standard, as she comprises 6,257,684 acres of wood-lands among her total of 25,659,266 acres. But it is a sheer impossibility to determine once for all upon such a general rule. The proper answer depends upon the purpose for which the question is raised. If it be intended to establish a normal proportion between the wooded and the not wooded area of a country in regard to its general culture, and especially to its climatic and agricultural conditions, much will depend upon the geological formation and situation of the territory. The fertile sites along the shores of the oceans need no woods, as the air currents laden with moisture from the sea regulate, in the most beneficial way, the climate of such country, and the easy access of vessels from all lands secure the importation of whatever wood is wanted. Just the reverse is it with mountainous regions. There nature itself has necessitated a much larger percentage of wood-lands than the above named, while in the broad plains of the interior of a large country that percentage might be sufficient to retain the good effects of forests, especially if they are properly distributed over the country.

But if the question be how to determine the portion of the wood-lands of a country to the not wooded areas, in order to raise a quantity of wood for fuel, timber and lumber, sufficient for the wants of the inhabitants, the proper answer cannot be given without the help of a statistical bureau for forest matters.

The duty of such a bureau should be to ascertain the quantity and quality of the wood which annually can be cut without injuring the sustained growth of the forests, and to compare this amount with the demands of the population for the different kinds of wood. If the country be able to meet the requirements of the inhabitants, we call the proportion adequate, otherwise there must be importation.

Entirely excluded from the question regarding the proportion of the wooded area of a country to the not wooded are the so-called "protective or shelter-forests," *i. e.*, such as would, when cut down, cause irreparable damage to the public. These forests, which will be treated of in the next chapter, must be preserved at all events, and be managed in the public interest.

CHAPTER IV.

RELATIONS OF GOVERNMENTS TO FORESTS.

THE necessity of forests to the permanent welfare of the commonwealth on one hand, and the rapid destruction of the woods by private owners on the other, led in the old world many economists to the assumption that it would be better for the prosperity of a state if all forests were owned, or at least controlled, by the governments. To the American mind this view seems incredible, as our opinions regarding the administration of private property are just to the contrary. We insist upon the least interference from public authorities with the management of private property. But when we consider that the benefits derived from the forests consist not only in revenues drawn from the forest vegetation, but also in the advantages bestowed upon the development and prosperity of the country by the influence of the forests in regard to climate, weather, protection of the soil, regulation of the flowing waters, etc., we cannot deny that *certain forests should be considered as public entailments*, given to us for our own use with the direction to transfer them in the best possible shape to the generations that will live after us, and who will, like us, be compelled to make the same use of their beneficence.

For this reason it is claimed that the State should own: (1) The forests and areas surrounding the watersheds of the navigable rivers and their tributaries, in order to secure to the country a continual and undisturbed water supply, on which not only depend navigation and commerce, but also agriculture and manufacturing industries.*

(2) The sand-downs or dunes along the sea coasts and all infertile tracts containing shifting sands which endanger the adjoining fertile lands, unless kept continually in wood.

(3) Every area unfit for agricultural purposes, but well adapted for forest culture, if the owner should not be able or willing to plant forest trees thereupon.

* The adage, "the forest waters the farm," is not a mere saying; it is undeniably true that without a proper management of forests in civilized and densely populated countries no remunerative agriculture is practicable; nay, without a proper preservation of certain forests, none of the several branches of the politico-economical household of a people can be in a prospering condition.

If this theory be accepted as correct, and justified by the principles governing our law in regard to the right of eminent domain, at least the claims sub 1 and 2 would bring the entire sea coast of our State, the Adirondacks, and Catskill mountains, *under the control of the State,* those mountains enclosing the head-waters of nearly all principal rivers of our State, especially those of the great Hudson River. The forests belonging to these first two classes are called "protective forests," because they have proved necessary for averting irreparable damages, which would befall the commonwealth if they were cut down at once. In the interest of the public welfare and the general culture of the countries, the European governments have obtained, if not the full property, at least such control of those classes of woods as to force the owners to manage their property without hurting the public interests. Should the present policy of our State Government, outlined in Secs. 7, 8 and 9 of the Act passed May 15, 1885, be strictly enforced, there is a good prospect that the Empire State in due time will be the undisputed owner of the denuded wood-lands in the higher regions of the Adirondacks. These lands are only capable of bearing—if anything at all—slowly growing forest trees. As the expenses of reforesting such tracts would far surpass the income derived for several generations to come, it is easily understood how private owners are inclined to abandon such property, allowing the State by tax sale to come again into possession of lands, the ownership of which never ought to have gone to private parties.* The State can safely take in hand the replant-

* The State of New York has also had the advantage of formerly owning most of the wood-lands in the Adirondacks. But the particular notion, entertained still by our Federal Government, that public lands, without much discrimination in regard to economic value to the country, should be disposed of as quickly as possible, led to the complete sale of the most beautiful wooded tracts, at prices ranging between five

ing of those lands, as it is not looking upon the forest products as a source of immediate profit, but upon the important economic effects which well cared for forests of this kind contribute to the general weal and prosperity of our country. Moreover, there is no doubt that the State, by introducing a systematic cultivation and exploitation, will be enabled to cover—without prejudice to the sustained growth of the woods—the actual expenses incurred in the difficult operation of reforesting the denuded areas of the high mountains.

In this connection it may be proper to call the attention of the reader to the difference between net proceeds obtained in a business which is conducted by a private party, and that which is managed by the commonwealth. The general economy of a people, it is true, consists of the total of the households of the single individuals, but this fact does not justify the conclusion that the highest success with the former is attained when the net proceeds (or rents of the soil) in the management of the private households have reached the highest point. For the determination of what are considered expenses incurred by the production is different in the two kinds of management. While the private person puts every expenditure for the production to the debit account of his business, the management of public property considers only such disbursements as real expenses (*i. e.*, as diminution of its income) as do not afford an immediate benefit to the people. For instance, if a private person possesses a mine which cost every year $100,000, in order to obtain its yearly output, valued at $100,000, there is no net profit, and the owner of the mine would hardly be inclined to

---

and ten cents per acre, with easy terms of payment at that. Both houses of the last Legislature passed a bill empowering, with certain restrictions, the Forest Commissioners to buy up wood-lands situated in the Forest Preserve at figures not exceeding $1.50 per acre. This bill has now become a law.

continue the enterprise, unless prompted by the charitable desire to give some men employment. From a quite different standpoint would in this case the question of the profitableness be considered, should the government take this work in hand. The $100,000 paid for labor, machinery, etc., would then be looked upon as benefiting the people, and the nation would have by the continued exploitation of the mine a profit of $100,000 every year, that being the sum which had been distributed for labor, etc. The same principles govern the profitableness of State forests, unless a State is forced or willing to use them as a source of revenue. If after all expenditures and receipts there be a surplus, all the better. But even if, after paying the salaries of the officers, the wages of the laborers, the cost for cultivating, planting, etc., nothing of the receipts be left, those items would not be regarded as expenses in the same sense as a business man would view them, but would represent a real gain for the commonwealth. In other words: owners of private forests endeavor to obtain from their property the largest possible income; whereas the managers of State forests should aim at the highest possible gross amount of revenue from the wooded public domain.

The advocates of state socialism use this maxim for justifying their theorem that every business which is carried on with the intention of accumulating wealth, should be conducted by the government or public authorities, and all net proceeds should be distributed among the employees. But in the public economy the natural principles are only effective and applicable as far as they are not modified by such laws as are acting alongside with them, or which are even opposed to them. In our democratic republic the doctrine that the State must only interfere "to protect freedom of labor," is in regard to the social question considered a corner-stone of our government, and therefore we do not allow the public authorities to undertake any enterprises, except such as are necessary for the promotion of the public welfare; and to this certainly belongs the care of the areas which secure to our navigable rivers a constant flow.

As for 3, the time has not yet arrived with us, in which we have to be so sharply on the lookout for utilizing every piece of land. But it is not to be denied that something should be done to make useful the 3,526,030 acres of the State lands which are by the last census registered as wild and uncultivated. This area comprises *more than one-eighth of the entire territory of the State*, is mostly hilly or mountainous, has been stripped of all trees by their owners, and, after having been used for a few years as pasture, became barren by the sun, which burnt the grasses up, and by the rains, which washed the fertile surface soil down the hills. There is no doubt that were these three and a half millions of acres planted with forest trees, the country would receive a great benefit, and by a proper management, the lands would yield a satisfactory revenue.

However, this does not furnish the State with sufficient reasons for exercising its right of resumption by eminent domain; but there is a good opportunity for the Croesuses of our country to combine business with beneficence toward the people. For whoever is able to spend 100,000 dollars without being compelled to look eagerly for any revenue from this money during the next generation, can make no better investment and bequest to his heirs, than to buy up large tracts of the wild lands in our State, and plant forest trees thereupon. By a sound systematic management, the purchaser may safely expect that in the course of time the net proceeds of his investment will *at least* equal the amount he would receive, if the invested money was entrusted to a savings bank. In the "old world" large tracts of forest lands are principally selected as family entailments, both on account of the safety of such investments, and the increase of the revenues in the future time. With us, entailments, containing provisions beyond the second generation, are against the law. But, unless the Legislature should find it advisable to exempt this special case for economical reasons from the general rule, the members of a family in a corporative capacity could attain the desired object, and the very rich men could in this way provide for their posterity, and at the same time benefit their country and fellow men. There are in the State of New York many hundreds of thousands of acres of sandy lands which scarcely return the cost of cultivation for agricultural operations. For five acres of sand need five times more outlay than one acre of good land, they require nearly five times as much seed and manure as one acre of good land, but they yield not a larger crop than the one acre of good land; in other words, sandy lands, or such infertile lands as are deficient in the principal constituents of a fertile soil, do not pay at all to the farmer, because to fertilize them, there would be involved more expenses than in the purchase of the most fertile grounds. An exception could only be stated, if the farm be situated in the vicinity of a large city, where additional manure can be procured cheaply, and where the farm products can be sold at a much higher price than in the distant country. Were all the unprofitable sand lands in our State to be planted with forest trees, the owners of them need fear no more disappointments in regard to the crops of sandy soil, but could confidently hope that the future would reward their efforts; under all circumstances they could be assured that their forest planting was a permanent improvement to the farm, and would show its full value at a sale of the farm, this being the time when *every* farm improvement is realized financially.

CHAPTER V.

ASSISTANCE FROM THE GOVERNMENT TO FOREST CULTURE—ESTABLISHMENT OF FOREST SCHOOLS FOR TRAINING FORESTERS.

THE American theory of State activity does not favor any system of a paternal nature. We therefore would not be inclined to encourage forest growing by awarding premiums or other pecuniary benefits to those who undertake the restocking of their denuded woodlands. However, there can be no doubt that it is the duty of the government to furnish the facilities by which the citizens may acquire the necessary knowledge for enabling them to secure all the advantages which arise from the scientific treatment of forests.

This view on the subject has been taken by our Legislature and framed in Sect. 18 of the Forestry Act as follows:

"The forest commission shall take such measures as "the department of public instruction, the regents of "the university and the forest commission may approve, "for awakening an interest in behalf of forestry in the "public schools, academies and colleges of the State, and "of imparting some degree of elementary instruction "upon this subject therein."

If this provision were carried out, the Empire State would inaugurate a new era in political economy, and would lay the foundation upon which to build the science of systematic forest culture. Then we would be inspired with the hope of having called into productivity the 3,526,030 acres of wild lands lying within our State, and which do not contribute one tithe to its wealth. Experience teaches us that in whatever country profitable and systematic management of the forests has been successfully introduced, the first step to it was the establishment of schools of forestry. For men educated in such schools become not only fit for their vocation, but consider their position as a trust, and perform their duty to the Government, instigated not only by their fealty to the public authorities, but by a professional pride which makes dear to them the forests given to their care and protection. From unskilled, hired men you cannot expect such devotion to the interests of the position as is developed in the trained forester. That man will always do his full duty even at the peril of his own life.

Whether our public schools are the proper places for awakening interest in behalf of forestry, we will leave out of this discussion, but our Agricultural Colleges should consider it incumbent upon them to impart not only elementary but full scientific information upon this subject. By pursuing this course, they would follow the example of similar institutions in European countries a century ago. For although it is true that in matters pertaining to forest culture much depends upon experience, and that the first impulses to an improved management of forests were given by practical woodsmen, systematic forestry did not make its appearance until the learned men at the universities took the matter in hand, and applied the principles derived from mathematics, natural philosophy, political economy and public law to forestry. After having found the teachings of the practical foresters to be in harmony with the principles of science, the learned men did not stop work, but continued their efforts to improve the method of managing forests, and built up a system of managing forests, which, although it cannot be declared yet perfect, has contributed much to the amelioration of the economical condition of the European nations.

Prominent teachers in forest culture are still at variance in regard to the aims and ends of their endeavors, but all concur in this that *Experimental Stations are neces-*

sary to help science in determining the correct methods of managing the forests advantagously and successfully. In Europe, colleges of forestry and agriculture are mostly combined, and require two years of study to complete the forestry course alone. During six of the winter months instruction is given in the several branches of forest science, while the summer months, after deducting some weeks for vacations, are employed in making excursions to places where forest operations are going on, or where the students have an opportunity to practise what they have learned during the winter time. The full winter course gives instruction in :

(1) Cultivation of the forest trees and the uses to which their woods may be applied, with the mode of propagating them upon different soils ;

(2) Forest exploitation and the managment of forests according to the various systems now in use ;

(3) Forest taxation and mensuration ;

(4) Surveying, draining, and embanking ;

(5) The methods of resisting the encroachments of shifting sands ;

(6) Care and chase of game ;

(7) Laws and regulations governing the forests.

For practising these studies, excursions are arranged during the summer months, and the students are trained in making topographical sketches, surveyings, openings of roads through unbroken forests; and in every kind of forest operation, which may occur either on plains or mountains.

The examination, which the candidates for appointment to a position in the management of forests have to undergo, is very strict, and the result of this system has proved eminently beneficial to the European forestry interests.

But of much greater advantage would it be at present for our State to establish a simple forest school in which young men could receive the proper training for rendering them fit for the position of foresters. The French government has done much to educate good foresters by purchasing the well known forest-farm "Barres," which is situated 1,000 feet above the sea level near the great Orleans forests. This farm had been used already for fifty years as a private Experimental Station for forest trees. The objects of this Station were:

1. Investigations in regard to the most profitable use of certain soils for raising the most valuable kinds of wood thereupon. With this department there were connected experiments for acclimatizing useful foreign forest trees.

2. Raising at the least possible expense the greatest amount of good seedlings, combined with observations in regard to the yearly increase of wood in the various forest trees.

3. Producing and closely examining the seeds used in the State forests.

The French government bought this farm in 1873, notwithstanding her great financial trouble at that time, for the purpose of establishing there a Government "*school of forestry.*" This was done without interfering in any way with the objects to which the farm had been during half a century so beneficially subservient. There was simply added to this establishment the "*school of forestry,*" in which young men obtain such information as to enable them, after the completion of the full course, to act as foresters. The course lasts through two years and is more calculated for a practical instruction than a high scientific education. To impart the latter, and to raise the higher officers in the department of forestry, the widely known Institution at Nancy is destined, and considered amply sufficient for all France. At "Barres" instructions in certain sciences are given only in order to accustom men brought up in common schools to concentrate their mental power more upon practical subjects. Therefore, only during four winter months is *elementary*

enlightment given to them in mathematics, geometry, surveying and leveling, forest botany, zoölogy and entomology, while they are thoroughly instructed, first, in the management of forests, with special reference to both the artificial and natural restocking of forests; and second, in the laws and regulations by which the administration of forests is governed.

The institution at Barres is a public one. A certain number of young men between the age of nineteen and twenty-four years are received every year, and after two years of study, having passed the examination, get an appointment for the lowest position among the forest officers, advancing to higher positions after some years' service and having passed further examinations. The pupils are, similar to our West Pointers, educated entirely at public expense, receiving even a small salary as pocket money. But they have during the eleven working months of the year—one being devoted to rest and vacation—to perform every manual labor required on the farm in cultivating the soil, raising seeds and seedlings for nearly free distribution among the French farmers, and all other work connected with the Institution. Besides this, they have to do every kind of labor in the adjoining State forests, which is needed to preserve the woods and retaining them in a first-rate condition ; they, therefore, have to personally do the seeding, planting, thinning and cutting of trees, making roads, openings, ditches, etc., in order to learn practically every work that may occur in the course of systematic treatment of forests, as these will come under their care and guidance.

To establish in or near the Adirondacks a school like this one, would be a move in the right direction for bringing into effect the well-meant instructions of the cited Section 18 of the Forestry Act. It is true that the Report on Forestry published at Washington in 1884 recommends very strongly the establishment of schools of forestry by the Federal Government, but to wait until this sensible advice should be acted upon, would show too much faith in the activity of Congress regarding affairs other than those merely political.* It is entirely a matter for each separate State in the Union to take care of its forestry interests and to educate its own officers, the more so as diversity of climate, situation and other economic reasons will make the proper training of the foresters in the various States in certain respects a diversified one.

As for the cost of establishing and maintaining such an institution, it would not be very large, especially if adjoining States of similar climate and topography would unite, and contribute in proportion to its support. In fact, the labor performed by the young men of the Institution would make it nearly self-supporting, and the demand for trained foresters in the United States would bring more students to the Institution than could be accomodated. But the benefit which the commonwealth would derive from the introduction of a systematic treatment of the State forests would be so great as to make it

* In the First annual report of the Ohio State Forestry Bureau for 1885, p. 20, we find the following well founded complaint on this point:

"When a few years ago the St. Paul, Minn., Chamber of Commerce petitioned the Congress of the United States to establish a National School of Forestry at St. Paul, the subject of *forestal education*, and more especially its necessity in this country, was discussed by the friends of forestry.

"Five years have elapsed and many of the warm advocates of the project have died. The subject seems to have been stricken from the programme of subjects at forestry conventions; the press too is silent on the question, and yet the subject has lost none of its great importance. No one who has studied the extent, the distribution and condition of our forests, and who has inquired into the prospet of a renewal of our forests, will hesitate to assert *that the need of instruction in forestry is an absolute necessity*.

"The objection that there is no need of trained foresters in this country, which was urged some years ago, was not based upon a knowledge of the extent and true condition of our forests, but rather upon a blindness to the best interest of our land."

nearly impossible to give at present a faint idea of its value. Besides a considerable income to the State, the army of laborers who are now used by unscrupulous lumbermen and their agents in illegally cutting timber on the State lands, and who are becoming every year more depraved on account of the unpunished continuance of their public plundering, could then be made to return to an honest and well paid activity, as a great many hands would be required in bringing the State forests into such a shape as to produce the largest possible output.* The moral standard of the laborers living in or near the State forests would rise again to the level of honesty, and the *"State Troops"* or *"The Grenadiers"* † would give up their dishonest ways and become

* Although the work to be performed in the management of forests does not require so many hands as in the management of farms, there is always so much to do that most of the laborers, who have settled in the sparsely populated wood countries, can find profitable employment. In Germany, the management of the forests is so conducted that a tract of from 40,000 to 80,000 acres of wood-lands—the greater number of acres being alloted to the mountainous regions—is given to the care of an "*Over-forester.*" This territory is divided up into *districts*, containing from 6,000 to 10,000 acres each, and superintended by a "*forester.*" Each of these districts is cut up into smaller tracts of from 3,000 to 4,000 acres, and placed in charge of an "*Under-forester,*" who superintends the laborers working within the tract. The number of common laborers employed during the most part of the year in the territory of an Over-forester is from 200 to 300. The average expense amounts to about one dollar per acre a year, while the average income runs to between two and three dollars per acre, leaving a net profit of from one to two dollars per acre. At the same time the condition of the woods is steadily improved, this insuring even a greater profit in the future. As most of these wood-lands are not fit for agricultural purposes, it cannot be denied that from this management a handsome revenue is derived, besides furnishing ample sustenance to thousands of families.

† The N. Y. St. F. R.. page 28, describes this class of men as follows: "Hidden within the remote seclusion of the wilderness, this latter class (of wood thieves) have been secure from observation, and there has been to a certain extent a banding together for defense and systematic plundering. This has become a matter of notoriety, so much so that in certain localities these organized bands of trespassers go by the name of "State Troops," while in others they are known as "The Grenadiers."

employees of the State. They would lose nothing financially by this change, while the money which formerly went into the pockets of the unscrupulous dealers in the stolen State property would flow into the State Treasury. The price for logs which now, owing to those nefarious operations, has sunk far below their real value, would rise to such a degree as to give to the owners of the woodlands encouragement for introducing a systematic management of their forests, from which in the future an adequate and permanent revenue would be derived.

CHAPTER VI.

FOREST PLANTING — PREPARATORY AND PRECAUTIONARY MEASURES.

In order to obtain all the advantages of real forests, the principal requirements are correspondingly extensive areas. Forests have to protect not only themselves, but also their surroundings against the atmospheric influences, and if a small forest shall perform this and contribute to the welfare of the country, it has to be brought into a proper connection with other wooded tracts. A forest will not have been built up satisfactorily, unless each tree is capable to protect his neighbor, and each wood lot is enabled to afford protection from sun, rain, wind and cold to the adjoining one. Only after this has been accomplished can a forest reach that state of perfection which is necessary to make it profitable and of economic value. To the simple farmer, who is governed only by his personal interests, a tract of from 10 to 20 acres may suffice for raising forestal products, especially if there is a protected situation, and a regular rotation in cutting and reproducing the forestal vegetation; but this is a *wooded tract*, and cannot be called a *forest*.

Precaution is everywhere advisable, and nowhere it is more necessary than in reforesting denuded wood-lands, because there not only come up considerations of the most complicated sort, but because mistakes committed in the execution of the plans often involve irreparable damages. It is very natural that those who undertake reforesting vast tracts of land, desire to complete their labors as quickly as possible, in order to be able to soon enjoy the fruits of their endeavors, especially if unlimited means are at their disposal. But if such improvements are to produce real benefits, large expenses should be avoided, leaving to the effect of time—and this is the most potent factor—the accomplishment of the most permanent benefits. Exorbitant expenses are in such operations never compensated for by what is gained in the shortening of time, whereas going ahead gradually, considerately and practically, will always bear good fruits.

For the same reason the area to be restocked during a certain season should not be too large. That the means of performing the proposed task must be adequate, is a matter of course. But before beginning to restock those parts of a large forest which are denuded and over which parching winds sweep unchecked, the old wooded tracts should be looked after, and if necessary, extended so that they are brought into a certain connection with isolated places of a large denuded area. Thereupon, when the work is to be entered upon, it should, if practicable, be commenced at a place which is already protected by the borders of adjoining woods. From there the plantation is pushed forward under the protection of the growing trees, until the whole tract is restocked.

If the site is entirely open, and blasting winds peremptorily prevent the growing of trees, there have to be protective earth walls thrown up, on top of which less valuable, but more hardy trees, such as poplars, cotton-wood and birches are planted. Under cover of this protection the planting may be begun, and if properly done, will prove successful.

In restocking large areas, a good deal of mental work must be performed before the undertaking can be commenced. Elaborate plans have to be made in which the lots, with proper divisions and sub-divisions, must be determined upon, roads and ways laid out, drainage attended to, in short, every thing must be considered which will assist in securing the vigorous growth of the trees. In making these plans, the limits placed by the necessity of returning the invested capital with compound interest, must never be lost sight of. Nor can we make use of any artificial fertilizer, for we have to be contented with the resources furnished by the kindness of nature. Therefore, first of all, we have to look for the dormant forces of nature, and to consider whether, and with what means, we may be able to make them subservient to our purpose. The agriculturist is able to correct his mistakes every year, but the forest culturist's mistakes accompany him to his grave, and often cannot be corrected, except by generations that come after him.

CHAPTER VII.

THE METHODS OF CULTIVATING DENUDED WOOD-LANDS.

THERE are several modes of cultivating wood-lands. To determine upon one or the other of them by a general rule or by theoretical principles is absolutely impossible, because everything therein depends upon the condition of the soil, climate and situation of the tract to be wooded. The only general rule which intelligent foresters follow in such cases is: first, to make a calculation in regard to the profitableness of the operation, and then to do the work as thoroughly as the means on hand will permit.

Before entering upon active operations, there should be taken into consideration everything influencing the growth and thrift of forestal vegetation. In this respect we have first to examine the condition of the soil, this being a source from which the *young* trees receive their principal nourishment. As the soil, especially on the plains, changes very much in regard to both its mechanical character and chemical condition of fertility, a close investigation of the components of the soil is required, to find out the quantity and quality of the plant-food contained therein.

Trees strive to penetrate with their roots as deep as possible into the soil. The more room there is for the extension of the roots, the more they will be developed and able to promote a quicker and stronger growth of the trees, these receiving a great deal of their food—and a very essential one at that—through the roots from the contents of the soil. Poor soils as well as exhausted ones offer great difficulties for raising trees, and, therefore, preparatory operations have to be undertaken, in order to enable them to produce a good forest vegetation. The obstacles to a vigorous growth of forest trees are manifold. *Sometimes* the soil, by the continuous and unimpeded exposure to the sun's rays and parching winds, has become thoroughly dried up and impoverished, and in addition to this it is often covered either on its top or in its intermediate layers with impenetrable strata of carbonaceous or feruginous substances, which prevent the growth of plants upon them. Sometimes the fertile soil has been either washed away or made too compact and firm, or swampy, or boggy, by rain or snow. In all such cases the soil should be brought, by proper plowing and subsoiling, into such a condition that plants will grow there. The soil having been deeply broken and mixed up with the macerated hard pan brings the hidden treasures of the deeper soil, consisting of easily soluble salts, carbonates or oxides, in contact with the fertilizing power of light and air, thus restoring the plant-food that had been washed down into the all-absorbing subsoil. Besides this the deep and thorough pulverizing of the impoverished soil increases the depth of the ground to which gases and humidity from the open air may penetrate, helping the growth of plants by increasing the warmth of the soil, and thus giving a more regular moisture to the roots of plants, both by supplying it in times of drouth and by carrying it away when in excess. Deep plowing of the ground is unavoidably necessary, if it is intended to plant forest trees with long tap-roots on heavy compact soil, as these trees will never have a vigorous growth, unless the soil is rendered fine to a considerable depth.

On heaths deep cultivation destroys the growth of lichens and breaks up the hard pans, both of which are heavy drawbacks to forest planting on the infertile heaths. The carbonaceous soil is entirely insoluble and impenetrable. It can only be rendered fertile by breaking and mixing it with the other ingredients.

The same favorable effect is accomplished with peat or muck soils. Stirring them up thoroughly to the depth of about 12 to 14 inches renders them able to produce valuable forest trees.

Forest vegetation cannot succeed but on soil which contains sand, clay and lime, the two first named being the most potent factors of vegetable growth. If the soil does not contain at least some parts of each of the three named minerals, complete infertility will be the result. The more equally these three ingredients are mixed together in the soil, the more fertile it will be. Nature has distributed these three minerals pretty equally all over the earth. But on many places they are not mixed together and, therefore, we have to apply deep culture in order to produce in the seed-beds the mixture wanted for a successful growth of forest trees. The only exceptions are the places where high winds have gathered and piled up the loose sands. These never must be touched by any means of culture, except by those which will be explained further below, and which confine themselves to means which never disturb the soil. The same is true in all cases where a layer of quick-sand is underlying a thinny surface clay soil. Here the cultivation should be confined to a slight stirring up of the fertile soil, leaving the infertile subsoil entirely untouched, otherwise the latter would be brought to the top and completely bury the fertile soil.

On tracts where the full deep cultivation of the soil is advisable and practical, certainly it is the better plan to undertake the operation to its widest extent. But as there exists on heaths great danger from shifting sands, and on mountainous declivities from washing away the soil by rain storms and snow drifts, it is often expedient to undertake those improvements in instalments, subjecting only parts of the whole tract to the appropriate treatment.

CHAPTER VIII.

CULTIVATION OF SOILS.

The implements for cultivating the soil with regard to forest planting are the plow, spade and hoe. Manual labor has great advantages on account of its thoroughness ; but the high price for labor forces us to mostly use plows, except in places where the condition of the soil (boggy, stony or steep) prevents the application of this useful implement. As a rule the double plow is used to break up larger tracts of denuded wood-lands, because it is only with such a plow that the heavy swath formed by a thick cover of lichens can be thoroughly peeled off, while at the same time the main plow enters deep into the soil, turning it over in furrows. Heaths which have remained for a long time uncultivated, are liable to formations of hard pan within the extent of the fertile soil. Such layers cannot be broken except by steam plows. These should also be employed where the cultivation of extended tracts justify a larger expenditure. It is a well-known fact that steam plows perform this work not only cheaper than horse-power, but also more thoroughly and beneficially for the growth of trees. Owing to the greater celerity of the movements of the plow, and its long screw-shaped boards, the particles of the soil and subsoil are infinitely pulverized and mixed together. A common plow never could do the work so nicely.

After the soil thus having been prepared, it is necessary to give it a rest of a year or at least of an entire winter, in order that the air, moisture, warmth and frost may act upon the infertile subsoil, newly brought to the surface, and impart upon it the ingredients which are missing in the subsoil, and yet necessary for a healthy growth of forest vegetation. At all events plantations cannot be begun on places treated in the aforesaid manner, unless the old turned under surface-soil has completed its fermentation and settling. After being exposed for some time to the air, the turned up subsoil will have lost most of its humic acid, and the insoluble mineralic parts of the same will have been partly made soluble, and for the roots of trees available; while the gases of the air, which have entered the soil, directly furnish to the plants vegetable food. Only after the soil has rested so long as to receive the said beneficial influences of its rest, planting may be successfully commenced.

The greatest difficulties in restocking denuded woodlands are encountered on the bare, steep slopes of the mountains, because every heavy rain carries away from there a part, if not every particle of the soil. Help against this trouble is found in seeding the places with quick growing, and, as to plant-food, unpretentious grasses, or planting such trees as will by their nets of roots bind the soil. On this mode of culture we shall treat in Part III.

CHAPTER IX.

DRAINAGE AND IRRIGATION.

The supply and the preservation of water in the soil is of the greatest importance to the growth of trees. Wherever drainage is required, there should at the same time be considered the question of preserving the humidity in the ground. By lowering the water table—*i. e.*, the top of the ground water, we always must prevent the exsiccation of the soil, if necessary, by the erection of some apparatus for stopping the flow of water at any desired time.

A proper quantity of humidity in the soil always exercises a beneficial effect upon the growth of trees, the roots of which only being able to assimilate the plant food contained in the soil, after this has been made liquid by the water. But stagnant water is detrimental to the growth of every vegetation : it kills the activity of the roots. In order to retain the proper degree of moisture in the soil of the plains, there should not only be had regard to the humidity received from the atmosphere, but also to the water contained in the subsoil, the ground water. The less rain is falling in the country, and the more the soil is liable to quickly evaporate its moisture, the more evident is the beneficial result of an abundant stock of water in the subsoil to the vegetation. In the not drained lowlands along the rivers, the water table is on the level with the river. But the moisture of the soil, owing to the capillary attraction, rises above this station so that the less is done in the way of drainage, the higher penetrates the humidity in those lands. This holds principally true in regard to swampy grounds or moorlands, which, owing to their sponge-like structure, are able to receive enormous quantities of water, and to retain it.

The injurious effects of wet soils to the growth of trees can easily be observed. Such soils are cold and do not retain warmth; whereas forest vegetation requires more than any other plant a warm soil. Moreover, a wet soil disolves the vegetable food contained therein rapidly, and carries it down into the subsoil, where it is inaccessible to the roots of young trees. Thus the upper soil is sometimes entirely washed out, losing a great deal of its power to sustain plant growth. An excess of moisture in the upper soil prevents access of air, and consequently there does not properly go on the *decomposition* of organic matter, nor the *disintegration* of the minerals contained in the ground, both chemical actions being necessary for the sustenance of plant life. When organic matter in the soil decomposes while in contact with an excess of moisture, there will be produced acetic acid and other organic acids, which soon make the ground sour. Then the formation of impenetrable layers of protoxide of iron will commence, and that means death to every vegetation. To the spongy, swampy soil, excessive quantities of water are especially deleterious, these swelling up the pores in the ground so greatly as to disturb the development of the tree roots, and causing, during the spring, late frosts.

A properly made drain leaves in moorlands enough moisture in their smaller pores for furnishing to the roots of young trees the necessary plant-food, helping at the same time to impact the roots in the soil ; while the air in the emptied large pores continues circulating, and neutralizes the acids produced by the moisture when coming in contact with the organic matter of the soil.

It is, therefore, obvious that in regulating the aqueous conditions of a tract of land, both the efflux and the influx of the water must be arranged so as to avoid the injurious effects of being too wet, and yet to retain in the ground the moisture necessary to plant vegetation.

In regulating the conditions of the water with swampy, boggy and peaty soils, an attempt should be made to bring fresh soil over the surface. This is done by digging parallel ditches of the proper distance, depth and width, and throwing the dug-out soil at both sides upon the thus formed beds. This culture, called border or bed culture (*Rabatten Kultur*), serves not only to improve the chemical but also the mechanical condition of the soil, and therefore has the same result as deep plowing has upon common soil.

The boggy or peaty soils especially require chemical improvement, as they mostly need the important substances for the growth of trees—the mineral components. For this reason they are unable to make their richness of nitrogen available to the trees, these being unable to appropriate the nitrogen, except after it has been converted, with the help of some minerals, into nitric acid. Besides, the spongy condition of this kind of soil does not furnish to the roots of trees the rest and stability necessary for the development of the root system, because the soil, in receiving humidity, swells up, and in drying up, contracts; thus always disturbing the position of the roots and preventing their development.

The improvement of peaty tracts can best be effected

by mixing sandy loam with them, especially when the latter contains marl, because such a mixture furnishes rich plant-food for the tree roots. But even coarse sand added to peaty soil would be a great improvement, because sand contains always a large part of silica combined with kali, which, either by the influence of the carbonic acid of the air, or of the humic acid in the soil, are disintegrated and converted into carbonate of lime, this being soluble in water, and in this shape available to the roots.

Moreover, this treatment acts beneficially upon the mechanical condition of the loose soil, which by the weight of the coarse sand is compressed, and yet remains porous enough to let the air percolate in the ground. Fine sand should not be used, because it never contains kali; in coarse sand kali always is found, and for this reason it deserves the preference.

Raising the soil by throwing earth over the surface of the borders (beds) is especially helpful in the regions of large rivers, where otherwise drainage is impossible.

The extent of the drainage, as well as the increase of the elevation of the borders, depends upon how much ordinary moisture shall be retained in the soil, and especially how high the water table in the subsoil shall rise. Upon common soil trees grow best when the ground water does not rise higher than 3 or 4 feet below the surface, because under such circumstances the superfluous water can run off, and at the same time the water evaporated on the surface soil can be easily replaced from the ground water through the capillary attraction. But the spongy peat soils, bogs, ferns, etc., attract, owing to their increased capillary functions, water too easily, and, therefore, must have a lower water-line than common soil.

We shall consider this question more fully, when further treating upon the drainage of swamps, bogs and peaty fens.

CHAPTER X.

THE SELECTION OF TREES.

If the question arises: What kind of trees should be selected for the reforesting of denuded wood-lands, the choice must necessarily confine itself to those trees which are indigenous to the given locality, and which afford ample protection to the soil against sun and wind. Wood-lands proper are commonly too poor, or have such a site as to render them unadapted for agricultural purposes; and even forest trees, although generally not being pretentious as regards soil, cannot prosper when very young, unless the surface soil contains some available plant-food. Therefore, the poorer the soil, and the more unfavorable the location, the more difficulties arise in answering the question: What kind of trees shall we plant in a certain locality? Then we can but look at such as will be content with poor soil, and these are the coniferous trees, especially the pines, as for instance: The Yellow Pine, Pitch Pine, Red or Norway Pine (*Pinus Austriaca*), and *Pinus sylvestris*, usually called the Scotch Pine. They not only lay the least claims on the soil as for plant-food, but with their leaves, broken twigs and decayed roots, give back what they have received from the soil, adding much to what they have elaborated from the atmosphere; thus they increase every year the quantity of the fertile surface-soil or *humus*, and perform this function nearly as good as the broad-leaved trees do. Besides, they are easier to raise than other trees, and as for the profits derived from their wood, these are at least just as large, as in raising other kinds of trees. Therefore, it cannot be denied that the conifers are the most desirable trees for the recuperation of the fertility of the soil in denuded wood-lands.

Of all the conifers there is no species which can compare in frugality quantity of wood production and returns with the Scotch Pine (*pinus sylvestris*). This tree, although a native of the Eastern hemisphere, is now largely grown here. It will succeed even upon the poorest soil, altering, during its growing period, the condition of the soil in such a manner that later on more valuable trees may me raised there. This species should always be resorted to in places where no other tree will grow, and although the benefits offered by it will not last longer than during its first growing period,—as it is losing its soil-shading capability after a growth of from 15 to 20 years—we cannot spare it, but have to give the plantation either a short rotation, or we must intermix other suitable trees right at the planting time, or later, as soon as openings in the plantation appear. In mountainous regions the Larch or Tamarack serves nearly all the purposes for which the Pine is used on the plains.

Excepting the general principles laid down in the preceding suggestions, there is no absolute rule for selecting the proper trees to be planted in a given locality. The best way to avoid mistakes is to study, not only the nature of the various species of the forest trees by themselves, and in aggregate life—but also the hints afforded by the lay of the land; and when we have mastered these hints, we should follow them by selecting such trees as will find on the given place everything that is required for their full development. At the same time we must not overlook *the purpose for which trees are planted*—a point which is to be considered even before the question arises: "What to plant?" For instance: When we advise the intermixture of spruces, oaks, and even beeches with pines, there could possibly some one find fault with us because the trees named will never reach a full development on poor ground, but become, after the first growing period, stunted and suppressed by the pines.

However, in giving this advice, our intention is accomplished as soon as those trees obtain a sufficient hold upon the soil to protect it against sun and air during that time in which the pine is unable to do this. The increased cost of the plantation, caused by the temporary growth of these trees, which will be removed before they have reached maturity, cannot be considered as a drawback, because the condition of the pines, these being the real stock of the plantation, will be so much improved as to fully counterbalance the additional expenses.

A more effective agent upon the amelioration of the soil can be made by spruces and firs. But these trees require more food for their sustenance than a poor soil is able to offer them, and they, therefore, cannot obtain a permanent footing upon it. Besides, the spruce, notwithstanding its desirability in an intermixture, does not preserve the freshness, that is: the vigorous activity of the soil, and, for this reason, should never be grown alone as a stock of trees. This fact might also account for the decaying of many blocks of the black spruce in the Adirondacks since 1878, of which the First Report of the N. Y. State Forest Commission, on pages 50, 62 and 76 complains.

The common beech renders very valuable services in the recuperation of the lost fertility to the soil, for it furnishes great masses of rich leaves, forming a vigorous humus-soil which is continually increased, and preserved in this state by the shading qualities of the tree. But as the beech requires for its luxurious growth a soil rich in soluble minerals, and as such soil will be claimed by the agriculturist, there will seldom be a chance for the beech to exercise its beneficial function, unless it be on mountainous slopes, where agriculture cannot be conducted.

Generally speaking, the densely foliaged trees, viz: Beech, Hornbeam, Spruce, Fir, Walnut, Chestnut are, in regard to the amelioration of the soil, to be preferred to those with thin foliage, as Oak, Maple, Ash, Elm, Birch, Alder, Aspen, Acacie, Pine, Larch, because the former furnish a continual cover to the ground, and create an always increased producing capability of the soil, while the latter, with their increased growth, draw for their subsistence more upon the soil, which, on account of the thin foliage of these trees, is continually decreasing in fertility, owing to its exposure to sun and air.

The greatest difficulties beset the forest-planter in the selection of trees to be planted, when denuded woodlands, and poor ones at that, in mountainous regions are to be reforested. Here we must not overlook the fact that, before the final stock of trees can be planted, often a cover of the ground has to be created by other easily and rapidly growing forest-trees. Under these, the young plants of the future stock of trees may be safely developed, until they are able to shift for themselves. An illustration of this is the Beech, Hornbeam, Fir, and other shade-enduring trees. These are, when young, so sensitive in regard to the influence of the sun and wind, that the seedlings, even upon the richest soil, will not thrive, unless shaded by densely foliaged trees.

The determination upon the proper trees to be planted on a given locality, should always be preceded by a careful examination in regard to soil, site, and surroundings of the place. As woody plants, except when very young, obtain the most part of their nourishment through the gases in the air, and not from the soil, it is obvious that the chemical conditions of the soil do not play such an important part in the development of trees, as is the case with grasses and other agricultural plants. But the mechanical or physical condition of the soil is of the greatest importance to the growth of forest trees, and, therefore, the investigation into this point should never be neglected. If such an examination is scrupulously conducted, it should lead with safety to the conclusion that the selected species of trees will find there everything which will secure its thrift. In doubtful cases those trees which lay the lesser claim upon the soil are to be preferred. The safest way is always to follow the hints of nature, and plant such trees as are thriving best in or near the region in which the planting shall be done.

This understood, we have still, as mixed planting now-a-days—and with the best reasons—is commonly preferred to the planting of pure stock, to determine upon what varieties will fraternize with each other when planted in a mixture. So, for instance, Elm and Maple do not agree with the Oak, Walnut and Hickory as neighbors, but will lean away, become crooked, and die out before reaching their maturity; whereas Ashes thrive well when planted with the last named trees. With such a mixture, the ground would be fully and profitably utilized, as the Ashes draw their food from the surface, and the other (tap-rooted) trees from the subsoil. Pines, although also provided with tap-roots, succeed very well in a mixture with Oaks, Hickories, Walnuts and Chestnuts; mostly, however, they serve as nurses to the last named trees, and are cut before reaching their full maturity, after which the sheltered trees obtain their full development. The Larch is often planted on suitable grounds as pure stock; but a slight intermixture of the common Pine or Scotch Pine has proven very advantageous.

It is very important for the forest-planter to know this behavior of the trees among themselves, and much remains to be done with us, to correctly classify the forest trees in this direction. Easier is another for mixed planting, also important classification of trees, viz: such as in their early age have a dense foliage, that, with increased age, is getting thinner, and such as preserve their dense foliage. To the latter belong Firs, Beeches, Spruces, and the Catalpa; to the former, Oaks, Birches, Pines, Larches, Hickories.

Valuable hints on mixed forest planting are given in the Report of the Division of Forestry, published by the Department of Agriculture at Washington, 1887, on page 189. There we read: "After having determined what kinds are desirable and suitable to be planted in a given locality, the possibility of mixing two or more kinds depends:

(*a*) On their relative capacity for preserving or increasing favorable soil conditions;

(*b*) On their relative dependence for development on light or shade; and

(*c*) On their relative rate of height growth."

As general rules for mixing are thereupon summed up the following:

1.—The dominant species, *i. e.*, the one that occupies the greater part of the ground, must be one that improves the soil conditions, generally a shady kind.

2.—Shade-enduring (*i. e.*, densely foliaged) kinds may be mixed together when the slower-growing kinds can be protected or guarded against the overshading of the more rapid grower, either by planting the slower grower first or in greater numbers, or in larger specimens, or else by cutting back the quicker-growing ones.

3.—Shade-enduring kinds may be mixed with light-needing kinds, when the latter are either quicker growing or are planted in advance of the former, or in larger specimens.

4.—Thin foliaged kinds should not be planted in mixtures by themselves, except on very favorable soils, as in river bottoms, marshy soil, etc., where no exhausting of soil-humidity need be feared, or else on very meager, dry soils, where most shady trees would refuse to grow, and one must make a virtue of necessity.

5.—The mixing in of the light-foliaged trees in single individuals is preferable to placing them together in groups, unless special soil conditions make the occupation of certain spots by one kind, which may be better adapted to them, more desirable, as for instance, the Ash in a wet ground (slough). When a slower-growing, light-needing kind is to be grown side by side with the quicker-growing shady one—as for instance, Oak and Catalpa—a group of Oaks will have more chance to withstand the shade of the densely foliaged Catalpa than the single individual."

The late Dr. John A. Warder, who was the first man in America to make an effort at developing a system of forestry adapted to this country, expressed his hopes, that we would in the course of time come to an expedient process for the care of our forests, dependent upon the correct answers of the question: Which trees should be planted in mixed groups, and which trees are obnoxious to one another? He observed that it is necessary to know respecting each of this species:

1.--The term of rotation of trees.

2.—The height attained by the trees at maturity.

3.—The rapidity of their growth.

4.—What trees should never be grouped together.

5.—What trees are exclusive, and should be planted in masses by themselves.

6.—Which require the protecting care of nurses.

From all this, appears the urgent necessity of establishing experimental stations in those parts of our country which are in need of the helping hand of the forester.

As far as my own experience in this State goes, I can

recommend the following mixture of the principal forest trees:

1.—Oaks with Ashes, Hickories and Chestnuts.

2.—Oaks with Spruces and Walnuts.

3.—Oaks with Pines and Spruces.

4.—Oaks with Beeches and Spruces.

5.—Larch with Pines and Oaks.

6.—Black Walnut with Maples and Beeches.

7.—Beeches with Maples, Elms and Ash.

8.—Black Ash with Alders and Beeches in swampy grounds.

9.—White Pine with Beeches and common Pines.

10.—Scotch Pine with Spruce and Fir.

11.—Locust, Ashes and Catalpa.

In our natural forests we find Birches scattered all over among groves of the various kinds of forest trees. However, we would not advise to mix this tree with other valuable ones, as the Birch, owing to the whipping property of its branches, injures, more or less, the young twigs and buds of the neighboring trees. Only to very poor soil and where no other trees but the Pine (on dry ground) and the Alder (on swampy ground) grow, we should assign the Birch.

CHAPTER XI.

THE VARIOUS SYSTEMS OF FOREST MANAGEMENT.

Wooded countries are unable to support a large population, as there is not mnch of the area left for raising the required grain, fruits, vegetables, etc. Therefore, increased population regularly diminishes the country's wooded area, increasing at the same time, the demands made upon the forest vegetation. Besides this, there are many other causes which often produce a sudden and enormous destruction of the woods, causing great destitution among nations, and heavy drawbacks to the progress of the general weal and culture of a people. The recuperative power of the forests being but slow, the human mind has long been bent upon inventing artificial means for the purpose of always having on hand a sufficient quantity of wood to satisfy the diversified demands of the public. This led to the introduction of a *systematic rotation* in cutting down the woods. The forests are divided up into as many if not equal but possibly equivalent parts,* as years are required to bring the trees to their *maximum growth,* and then every year one lot is entirely cleared of trees and thereupon replanted. The next year the same treatment is applied to the second lot, the third year to the third one, and so on until the whole tract is gone over. Then the trees on the first lot will have reached their full growth again, and be ready for the axe.

This mode was certainly a progressive one, and it is still in practical use in many of the European countries. But it often caused great inconvenience, when the lot to be cut contained trees which were not so much wanted as other trees, that grew upon lots not yet reached by the rotation. And then it was ascertained that the division of the forest alone in as many lots as possible, did not secure an equally sustained production through the successive cycles of the rotation, the second crop never being

* The reason why the woods are divided up in this way is to obtain, at every cutting period, an equal average product of the forest vegetation. As the various portions of a large forest, on account of difference in soil, exposure, etc., often vary very much in their productiveness, parts equal in extent are not always equal in production. To obtain such equivalence, it is necessary to take into consideration the variations in soil, in exposure, and in adaptation to the growth of the kind of trees which happen to be upon it.

equal to the primitive, nor the third to the second, and so forth.

And then there arose a diversity of opinions relative to the ends and objects to be reached by rotations in forest culture, and this was the more important, as upon the decision of this controversy would depend the determination of the proper (that is, the most economical) time of the growing-period of forest trees. In this regard there prevail four different opinions, which are based upon the following principles :

1.—The principle of the uninterruptly continued production of the same kind of trees in a certain wooded area.—By putting into practice this principal, there will at the *same* place always be the *same* pure stock of trees, and as for their cutting time, those periods will be observed which will secure the continuance of the original stock.

This system, called the *block* system, and worked in rotation, was not long since the most popular in Germany, because it satisfied the national predilection for extended forests of *large* Beeches, Oaks and Evergreens. The growing periods for the single lots of the rotation were of long duration, viz.: from 120 years to 140, and even 200 years.

But the increased demands made by the industries for other kinds of wood, and the decreasing demand for the high-priced Beeches as fuel, on account of the inexhaustible supply of cheap mineral coal, shook the foundations of a system which had no regard for the wants either of the present or of the future. And then it was shown that the "sustained" production of the wooded area and its fertility could even be better retained by growing such kinds of wood as are now more in use—Ash, Maple, Elm, Alder, etc.—and that a growing period of from 60 to 80 years allotted to said modern trees, was financially much more profitable than the former large ones.

2.—The principle of the maximum growth of the trees.—In accepting this principle, the time of cutting the trees has arrived as soon as the yearly average increase of the wood in the trees has reached its highest point.

The average maximum growth of a tree is found by dividing the entire mass of the tree by the number of years of its age. The current or yearly increase of the mass shows the relation of the quantity of wood grown during the year in question, to the existing whole mass of the tree.

3.—The principle of producing the maximum of value. —According to this principle, the lot is cut as soon as the trees have reached the age at which they bring the highest prices in the gross amount. The average maximum of value is found in the same way as the maximum of growth.

But these two latter systems suffer the same fault of having their cutting periods too far apart, thus preventing the capital invested from being made profitable; for trees do not continually increase in their growth at the same rate in which the capital invested accrues with compound interest. They grow only during the first sixty or seventy years in a proportion adequate to straighten their debit account, and leave then a handsome profit. Later this proportion changes very much to the detriment of the capital. For instance: A forest of Conifers furnishes at the age of one hundred years not much more wood than double the quantity which it would have yielded at the age of sixty years, while the sum representing the value of the wood at the forest's age of sixty years, would, with compound interest, increase during the next forty years to at least *four* times its amount.

trees, although using an equal quantity of plant-food, abstract different elements from the soil and leave it in a much better condition in general than if only one kind of plant-food were exhaustingly consumed. Besides, the mixed stock of trees offer more opportunities to satisfy the growing demand for the various kinds of wood. Therefore, the scientific forest culturists of the present time have directed their efforts toward

(*e*) Introducing the so-called plenter-management. By this the primitive forest, in which the various trees are mixed up, both in regard to kind and age, is divided into a certain number of large tracts, according to the time required for the reproduction of the full-grown trees. But instead of confining the exploitation at a time to one of these tracts, the supply of wood required is obtained, during a certain period of years, from the *felling* of the trees in *one* tract, and from the several *thinnings* and other *necessary* cuttings *in others*. For instance: it is intended to treat, by this management, a wooded area, say of 50,000 acres, with different kinds of soil and trees of various ages, the full development of which would be reached by an average growth of 80 years. Then the forest is divided up into eight equal or at least equivalent parts, which are separated either naturally by roads, creeks, mountains, etc., or artificially by opening paths or roads that serve at the same time as a protection against fire, wind-breaks, snow-drifts, and as outlets for forest vegetation. During a period of ten years there are taken from one part * at different places, whatever timber, fuel or lumber may be wanted, thinning out at

---

* Those parts, in Germany called "Reviere" (Districts), are subdivided into lots of from 200 to 300 acres, which are also separated by paths from 10 to 14 feet wide, called "Schneisen." They have, like the wider roads of the Districts, proven very useful in suppressing forest fires and protecting the trees against wind-storms and snow-drifts, besides their principal use in serving as an outlet for the products of the forest.

the same time in other tracts those trees or bushes which encroach upon other trees, and felling such trees as have passed their maturity and are going to decay. The same operation is done during the next decade in the next tract, and so forth, till all the tracts are fully exploited, when the cycle of successive fellings will be recommenced again. These cuttings can, if desired, always be so arranged as gradually to arrive at groups of trees of the same age and description, and finally at blocks with high forest trees worked in rotation. At all events, the fellings are so conducted as to secure simultaneously and without prejudice to one or another part of the forest:

(1) A continually sustained supply of a desired variety of forest products.

(2) A sure reproduction of the forest, either by self-sown seed, by shoots and suckers from stumps and roots of felled trees, or by seeding and planting.

(3) A progressive and improved condition of the forest, in place of former deterioration.

In these three points there are concentrated the objects which scientific managers of forests in Germany and France have in view, and which are being accomplished, not there alone, but also in other European countries to which students of forest science have brought the knowledge of advanced management of forests. This revolution in the management of forests was brought forth by the calculations made in finding the exact amount of the net proceeds obtained from the usual forest exploitation.

The mode of ascertaining the proceeds of a capital invested in forest culture is as follows: The value of the lands and all expenses, from the time of beginning the plantation, or cultivation till the time of cutting, are figured up, and compound interest from the time of incurring the expenses till the cutting time is added. This sum forms the *debit account.* The credit account is made up by figuring all the revenue derivable from the forest during the growing period, and carrying it forward with compound interest to the cutting time. The value of the wood at the cutting time is found by the help of tables based upon certain methods of determining accretion in yearly mass, and large experience for every variety of wood in any kind of soil and location, and this amount, added to the sum of the revenues with compound interest, forms the *credit account.* If from this amount is deducted the total of the debit account, the difference is the amount of the net revenue. For instance: the 80 years' growing period for a certain plantation shows that the invested capital of $10 for an acre would yield, at the end of this period, a net revenue of about $154; while the 50 years' period by the same calculation netted $110; the 60 years', $125; 70 years', $130; 90 years', $140; 100 years', $130; 110 years', $120—the 80 years' period would be considered the most profitable, netting over four per cent. interest, and the others less.

The term "*Forest Gardening*" is sometimes understood to signify a special mode of systematic forest culture, quite distinct from the others now in use. But this phrase, correctly applied, means simply a plenter management made serviceable in certain localities, and under certain conditions. While the forester has generally to deal with the aggregate of trees in the woods, his attention is not infrequently claimed by single trees, or by groups or rows of trees, which serve to protect the soil from the influence of sun and air, and the neighborhood from the effects of sudden atmospheric changes. In such cases extraordinary measures must be taken to prevent, at all events, openings in the woods; the single trees have to be always watched, and those, which from overmatureness or other causes are incapable of affording effects which would justify their preservation, must be carefully removed and replaced by others of a suitable character.

This sort of forest culture is resorted to upon mountain summits, to retain the atmospheric moisture in the ground, and upon steep declivities, to prevent rains from washing down the soil and causing land-slides. It is also applied upon level plains, where areas of loose sand, if not retained by forest trees, may spread in sand-drifts and bury adjacent cultivated fields. Agricultural lands which are exposed to strong winds and frost, can be protected against these influences by surrounding them with the proper trees, disposed in screens or belts. This treatment is especially useful in small farms where a sustained growth upon the wood-plot is highly desirable, and for this reason it will be of practical benefit to us.

If from the foregoing suggestions it should appear desirable that an application of the methods above alluded to should be made to our wild or natural forests, it is evident that the so-called plenter management would be the best adapted to them. We are still in the fortunate position that we need not look out either for the natural products of the State forests, or for revenues derived from them; but we should make use of this opportunity and employ better and more efficient means to preserve our forests, than those which are calculated to protect them against fire and spoliation only. We should put an end to the present chaotic condition within the forests, and introduce a *methodical exploitation* of the woods, combined with a proper care for the undergrowth, so that the trees cultivated shall be such as are most adapted to the different localities of our widely dispersed state forest, and may satisfy the demands of the people for fuel, timber and lumber. Under expert management we can reach these objects, and at least make our forests self-supporting, provided that at regular intervals every harvested forest product is sold at public auction, and not

—as is now the practice—left to rot and create dangerous fire-traps, or breeding places for noxious insects.

CHAPTER XII.

RAISING FOREST TREES BY NATURAL REPRODUCTION.

SHOOTS.

THERE are a great many trees—to be found mostly among the deciduous varieties—which have the power of forming buds in the stem or exposed parts of the roots, in addition to the usual buds formed upon joints and the base of leaves.

The formation of these adventitious buds seems to be caused by the endeavor of the tree to apply to the production of new shoots the plant-food taken up by the unhurt parts of the root. These new shoots grow up into trees and are called coppice or copse-wood. Thus in a very simple way the restoring of forests has been made practicable by saving and properly treating the stumps and roots of felled trees. The more a certain kind of tree is inclined to coppicing, the better is this mode of propagation adapted to it, and it is a method which in many cases will be found to be the cheapest and most successful. In employing it, the cutting of the trees should always, if possible, be exactly even, and in an upwardly sloping direction, care being taken not to separate the bark from the trunk, because their conjuncture at the line of incision is the place at which the new shoots will appear. Experience shows that trees which can be propagated by sprouts, lose with their advancing age the capability of sending up vigorous shoots. We should, therefore, select the stumps of vigorous and younger trees for natural regeneration, and if these cannot be found, it is better to plant seedlings for coppice than to force old stumps to spend their last energy in sending out some weak shoots.

The condition of the soil, with respect to its being either dry, or wet and swampy, has an important influence upon the result of the operation. In the former case the trees should be cut close to the ground, so as to force the roots to produce shoots underground. The trees growing up from such shoots are more capable of standing drought than shoots produced on higher stumps. On swampy soil, especially if subjected to overflows, the stumps should be left high enough to prevent the water from overflowing them, because if cut too low, the stumps will sometimes be covered with water, and will perish for want of air. As that part of the old root, which produced the new tree, detaches from the old root system, forming a separate root with its own rootlets, there is no limit to the continued reproduction, provided the dead leaves, broken twigs, branches, etc., of the trees are left on the ground to decay, for they are the manure especially adapted to trees, and when taken away—as is often the case in husbandry, to serve as litter or feed—the woods, being deprived of a natural element of their thrift, exhaust themselves and dwindle away, while the soil of those forests, where the leaves are never removed, continually grows richer and yields better products.

If denuded and neglected wood-lands are to be restocked cheaply and quickly, the first step to be taken is to cut, in the manner described, every stunted tree or bush, and to smooth off the stumps where the surface is rugged. The best time for cutting trees, in order to raise coppice-wood, is during the dormant season, that is, during the latter part of the winter, or after the coldest weather is over. Trees should never be cut for this purpose later than March.

LAYERS.

Sometimes stumps develop shoots which may be bent down into the soil to a certain depth, after an incision has been made on the under side of the shoot, in the bend, so as to split it, if possible, a little below the bud, and to form a tongue. A hooked peg is usually employed to hold the layer in place. The tops should be elevated above the surface of the ground in an upward direction, and tied up to a pole. In time, the buried parts of these shoots (or branches) take root, and finally become individual trees. The ground around the layers should be kept quite clear of weeds, and the layers should be freely watered in dry weather. When sufficiently rooted the layers should be carefully separated from the stool (parent tree) with all the rootlets attached to them, and planted in nursery lines, or in those situations where they are permanently to remain. Layers may be made at any time in the growing season; but they will root sooner if made when the trees are growing rapidly (spring) than at any other time. The process of producing layers, as we shall see further on, is of great importance in replanting denuded side-hills where rain may wash away the soil. The roots of the old stumps and the new roots of the layers bind the soil, and thus prevent its washing out.

CUTTINGS.

While "shoots" are produced in deciduous trees by adventitious buds, the layers and cuttings of some of the deciduous trees have the power of forming roots. A number of trees can be propagated by cuttings, as for instance: the Willows, Poplars, some of the Alders and

R.S. Stoddard

Maples, and the Buttonwood or Sycamore. It is advisable to make these cuttings in the fall; they should be about twelve inches long, and made in wood of the current season's growth, and heeled, during the winter, in a moist place, protected against frost. This serves to form on the base of the cuttings a callus from which the roots push out, as soon as they are planted in the spring. They should be set deep enough to nearly cover their greatest part, and treated in the same way as transplanted seedlings, except that they should be set slanting —not straight. For when the ground settles it packs to the cuttings, and prevents them from becoming loose, a result, and a very injurious one at that, which often prevents the prosperous growth of straight-planted cuttings.

To promote the production of roots of cuttings which are planted in dry soil, they should during the summer months be mulched, as only a moist soil is able to secure the quick and strong development of roots.

Cuttings do not well stand transplanting. It is, therefore, advisable to set them where they are to remain.

Coniferous trees in general cannot be reproduced in the natural ways just named, but require the artificial means of propagation by seeding or planting. However, there is a natural way in which denuded wood-tracts, which had been covered with conifers, may be replanted, provided there are left at proper distances standard or parent trees, from the scattered seeds of which young plants can spring up. This treatment can be recommended as efficient with very poor soil where there is no danger of grasses easily getting hold of the ground. But if it is to be expected that such will be the case, a light tillage with a wooden harrow should be given to the soil in the late spring. By this operation the mosses and grasses spreading over the ground are destroyed, and the seeds which fell from the parent trees will be sufficiently covered in order to secure to the tract a natural regeneration. The standard trees, which serve as parent trees, are commonly called with us "staddles." One tree is sufficient for each intervening space of from 60 to 80 feet; for an acre of woodland from 10 to 12 seed trees would, therefore, be required.

In Europe the use of these natural modes of reproducing forest trees is exceptional, and is confined to particular localities and conditions. True, where a denuded wood tract contains a sufficient number of trees which will copse, and which have not yet reached an age when they can no longer send out vigorous shoots, coppice culture will invariably be resorted to. The skillful application of the planter management in the administration of the forests has been able, in time, to convert mixed coppice woods (or low forests) into middle forests, and even into high forests, with a pure stock of trees and the block system. But, usually, forest trees are now raised artificially, either by seeding or planting, which methods we will, in Chapters XIV and XV, consider in connection with the principal forest trees.

CHAPTER XIII.

THE COLLECTION AND TREATMENT OF SEEDS FOR FOREST TREES.

The easiest way of procuring seeds for forest trees is to buy them from the seed dealer. But as even the most conscientious dealer will seldom warrant the full vitality of his stock, it is a much better plan to gather them when ripe, and, unless used at once, to properly preserve them till seeding time. At all events the seeds should, before using them, be subjected to a vigorous test in order to ascertain the percentage of seeds which will germinate. For this purpose the forest planter should apply one of the many well-known modes of testing the germinating power of the seeds, and act accordingly. Seeds which show in the test that 70 per cent. of them sprout, are called good, whereas those which contain only from 50 to 60 per cent. kernels of germinating power, are called fair. Seeds which show vitality only in less than 50 per cent. should be rejected, if offered by the trade.

(*a*) SEEDS OF DECIDUOUS TREES.

The seeds of deciduous trees are easily collected. Most of them ripen in autumn, but a few, as Elms, Poplars, and kindred trees, some species of the Maple (soft Maple) produce mature seeds early in the summer, while seeds of Birch, Mulberry, and like kinds, ripen later in the summer.

The seeds should be sown as soon as they fall from the tree, because they do not keep well over till next spring. But if it is desirable to preserve them for later use they should be treated in the following way:

After the seeds have been collected they are subject to what is called "sweating." The seeds, or fruits, are for some time (about 8 days) gathered in a heap, and when signs of heating appear they are spread and dried till they become completely siccated. In order to accelerate this condition, the room in which the process of drying is carried on may be heated up to 90 degrees, provided care is taken for an abundant circulation of fresh air.

Cleaning of the seeds, and removing the different covers in which they are imbedded require special attention. A bag half filled with those seeds that are enclosed in dry shells, pods, or hulls, is beaten with a stick, and then the seeds are winnowed. Small quantities may be cleaned by hand.

Seeds having a fleshy and succulent cover must first be

denuded of it. This is done by squeezing the kernels out of the fleshy portion, cleaning them in water, and thereby freeing them from all fibrous and slimy parts. Then they are dried.

Winged seeds are usually slightly trashed with a stick, like those which have dry covers, but it is more safe to rub them with the hands, as even the slightest beating may destroy the vitality of the kernels.

Seeds with woolly covers (poplars, willows, etc.,) should be rubbed between the fingers. This can easily be done when the seeds, either by artificial or solar heat have been dried to such a degree that the adherent parts, by the touch of the fingers, can, without any effort, be separated from the kernels.

In regard to the preservation of the seeds of the principal forest trees, the necessary directions are given in the next chapter in treating of the seeding of the several kinds of forest trees. As a general rule it may be said here that most seeds of deciduous trees will be preserved over winter when mixed with sharp, moist (not wet) sand, and kept protected from the access of the atmosphere in a place not exposed to the cold and wet.

If large quantities of seeds of Oaks, Beeches, Hickories and other hard-shelled nuts are to be kept over winter, a kind of cellar should be made in the open field similar to the well-known potato cellar. A ditch about 7 feet wide and 2 feet deep is dug, and the earth taken out is used to build the side-walls of the cellar. Over these a roof is laid of straw, reeds, or sedges. In this cellar the nuts, after having been dried well, are piled up from 12 to 14 inches high, as soon as the cold weather sets in, and they should be shoveled over during the winter several times in order to prevent heating. The gable ends of the roof remain open till the strong frost commences, when they are closed with straw mats. The nuts will be well preserved in such a surface cellar, and will not lose their vitality, even should they show signs of sprouting in the spring.

(*b*) CONIFEROUS TREES.

Much more difficult, but also much more remunerative, is the collection of the seeds of coniferous trees. The cones, from which the seeds have to be extracted, should be collected at the time of their maturity. This time differs much with the various kinds. Hemlock, and *Abies alba* produce ripe seeds late in the fall, Larch and Spruce during the first winter, the Scotch Pine (*Pinus sylvestris*) matures its seed in the second winter. The exact time of the maturity of the cones should be rigidly observed, this period being near the time of the natural distribution of the seeds, the extraction of them is then greatly facilitated.

The extraction of the seeds in the cones is effected either by artificial or solar heat. The former mode is generally employed in Europe, as it is more expeditious and permits the making of larger quantities. In Sweden and Germany, the countries where this industry is most cultivated, there are erected on the ground floor of a stone building heating apparatuses, similar to those used in hot-houses, by which, from a circuit of pipes, heated air is conveyed throughout the room. In this room are constructed scaffoldings, on which may be placed trays of wooden lattice or wire-work, 5 feet long and 2 feet wide, in stages of about 6–7 inches between. Under the lowest range of trays drawers are placed to receive the seeds. The trays are then filled up three quarters of their capacity with cones, and the heat of the furnace brought to a standard of from 80 to 90 degrees. This heat is maintained till the cones open, whereupon the trays are shaken, commencing with the highest row, so that the seeds may fall from tray to tray till they reach the drawers of the lowest tier. When the cones beneath have opened as extensively as possible they are taken out and placed in a churn-like vessel with an opening, by which the seeds which have remained in the cones may pass, and be received in a wooden box placed beneath. The cones are then well shaken until completely emptied of their seeds, and the empty cones are employed to feed the fire in the furnace.

At some places in Germany they use, instead of these hot houses, ovens with iron plates on the tops, upon which the cones are placed, and by heat forced to discharge the seeds. This device is not to be recommended, as the plates very often become too hot, and the seeds are burnt and deprived of their vitality.

The extraction of seeds by solar heat is preferable to that by artificial heat, as the seeds thus obtained, never having been exposed to excessive heat, do not lose their vitality. When solar heat is to be employed, a framework or scaffolding similar to that just before described is placed against the wall of a building on a southern exposure. Upon this the trays are arranged of such a height between that the sun's rays may fall on all alike. Under the lowest trays are drawers provided with coverings of thick cloth, so that, if rain falls, the seed may be covered at once and kept dry. The whole apparatus is covered with a light roof, the slope of which runs toward the north. After the cones have been exposed for some time to the sun and summer heat they will open, and then they should be shaken, commencing with the trays in the upper tiers and proceeding in regular succession to those of the lowest row, whereupon the seeds are collected in the drawer. When the cones have opened as much as possible they are taken away and put in a churn, such as has been described above, for the extraction of the seeds which have remained in the cones.

If it is desired to divest the seeds of their wings, the

best mode is to put them into bags, filled only to one-half or one-third of their capacity, and thrashed slightly with a stick till the wings are separated from the kernels. The contents of the bags are cleaned by means of a winnowing fan.

The seeds of Evergreens can, without danger, be preserved for some years. In such a case they should not be separated from the wings. This preservation will be still more efficient when the seeds remain in the mature cones, and are extracted shortly before seeding time.

For our conditions the solar extraction of the seeds of Conifers is, undoubtedly, the most advisable mode, not only on account of the safety and cheapness of this process, but because the solar heat here is more lasting and powerful than in Sweden or Germany, and the quality of seed thus collected in this country would be the best imaginable.

In regard to the duration of the germinating power of the seeds of forest trees, many efforts have been made to ascertain the period of time during which the various seeds retain their vitality; but the results have been very unsatisfactory. It is only safe to say, that this period is with all kinds of these seeds comparatively a short one, but that most of the seeds of Conifers retain their germinating power longer than those of the deciduous trees, especially when left in the cones, or at best, when not separated from the wings, and carefully housed. However, the seed of Spruce, Cypress, Hemlock and Larch should not be used when older than one year.

The seeds of most of the deciduous trees lose their vitality after the lapse of one year, as, for instance, Oaks, Chestnuts, Maples, Beeches, Birches, while the seeds of the Locust, Arbor Vitæ, Ash, Mulberry, Alder, and Catalpa retain it for two years. Seed with a spongy or fleshy cover, as the Juniper, should be sown at once, when ripe, because their germinating power will be gone after the exterior hull has become fully dry.

The safest way, therefore, is always to use fresh seeds collected from the parent tree at the time of their maturity.

It has been stated as a general rule that seeds of plants when not collected in the locality, where they are to be planted, nor in a similarly conditioned locality, shonld be taken from a colder rather than a milder region. This rule holds good also for forest trees, and for this reason it is advisable that forest nurseries should be located in the vicinity of those woods for whose renewal they are destined.

CHAPTER XIV.

SEEDING FOREST TREES.

THE artificial regeneration of denuded wood-lands is effected either by sowing the seed of forest trees, or by planting seedlings. The production of seedlings is practicable only upon soil that is free from growing weeds or grasses, and entirely clear, so that there need be no apprehension that a grass cover will be formed during the first two years. In such cases, if good seed can be procured at a moderate price, seeding large tracts of woodland will certainly be cheaper than planting, besides the areas thus seeded will, by the process of thinning, furnish material for fuel or other purposes sooner than those that are set with plants; still, taken all in all, seeding is never as certain as planting, and as soil which is fit for seeding (*i. e.* free from weeds and grasses) is also suitable for the planting of two-year-old plants, and as such mode, by proper manipulation, requires little, if any, more expense than seeding, we would not recommend the latter for general culture, but would advise seeding only in nurseries to raise the material required for plantations. Therefore, in the following, we will consider first the beds upon which seedlings are raised, and then the nursery-rows into which the seedlings are transplanted and cultivated up to the time when they are to go to the grove or place where they are to remain permanently. However, after having given the instructions for seeding a certain kind of forest trees upon seed-beds, we shall briefly add the most usual and tried methods of using these seeds in the general culture of forest trees.

SEED-BEDS FOR THE PRINCIPAL FOREST TREES.

(*a*) *Seed-beds for Coniferous Trees.*

We select some place of good humus soil located on forest ground, with a protected situation, break it up in fall with the plow, divide it in beds of from five to six feet width, and leave it untouched during the winter. Should the soil be covered with heath-growth, or with a heavy grass sod, the sward must, previously to the plowing, be peeled off by the skim-plow, and entirely removed from the field, for, if plowed under, there would be formed in the ground, during the next year, such a thick net-work of fibres that the seedlings, when taken out for transplanting, would lose many roots and rootlets, these being kept in the grasp of the dense matting, and thereby broken.

As soon as the ground in spring has become moderately dry, the beds should be plowed once more and carefully harrowed. They are then ready for the reception of the seed. Four small furrows are formed the whole length of each bed by laying down a lath four inches wide, and pressing it into the ground by walking to and fro upon it. When taken up, a drill-row four inches wide is formed, the bottom of which offers a smooth, level ground to the seed for germination. The seed (in the proportion of about 20 to 30 pounds of winged seed to the acre) is then evenly and plentifully strewn into the furrows and covered loosely—not more than one half of an inch—with well-burnt sod ashes, mixed with some sand, or with compost. Good, fine humus soil taken from the woods may also be used, though this is apt to favor the growth of weeds between the plants—something that always should be avoided. A cover of clayey soil should never be applied, this being conducive to form, from rain or watering, a crust which prevents the seedlings from freely breaking through the surface.

To ward off birds, especially wild pigeons, from damaging the seedlings by eating the tops as soon as they appear above the ground, it is necessary to cover the beds with dry sedges and boughs—pines preferred, as spruce and hemlock drop the leaves too readily—until the leaves of the young plants have developed and thrown off the tops. In a dry season it is necessary to carefully water the beds in order to assist in the uniform sprouting of the germs; but great care should be exercised to prevent the soil from becoming crusted. Weeds should be entirely eradicated, and the ground between the drills well stirred up, a work which requires but little labor, if done in time. After every good weeding the drills should be filled up with some compost. Weeding and stirring the soil of the seed-beds should be entirely omitted late in fall, otherwise frost will hurt the seedlings. In the second year the young plants must, whenever the soil had been stirred up, be covered at the roots with some earth. After the lapse of two years—or if very strong plants are desired—after three years the seedlings are ready for transplanting, those of the common pine, white pine and larch being already, after one year's growth, fit for this operation. In the mountains the young plants are exposed to greater hardships than on the plains. There seedlings are not transplanted before they have reached the fourth or fifth year. They are then taken up in large balls and brought to the planting-ground, where they are carefully separated from the ball, and planted, as is described in the next chapter.

Some people sow broadcast upon seed-beds laid out four feet wide, and separated by small paths, using for the acre from 30 to 40 pounds of cleansed seed, that is, double the amount of seed required in drill rows. But this method cannot be recommended, as the cleansing of such beds is very difficult, and the seedlings, when they are going to be taken up, cannot be handled so carefully as when raised in drill-rows.

Seeding on a large scale is operated either with cones or seeds, the latter being either winged or unwinged. The cultivation of the grounds to be seeded down depends much upon the condition of the soil, as a loose soil requires less stirring up than a compact one. On very light soil, especially on heaths having only a very thin surface growth, or none at all, and on mountains with a very thin sward, no plowing should be employed; cross harrowing with the iron harrow is in such cases sufficient to prepare a good seed-bed. The seed is then properly distributed, and covered by dragging over the field with a brush-harrow—*i. e.* a wooden harrow, between the teeth of which twigs have been entwined, in order to prevent them from entering the soil.

Seeding cones on large tracts is now much recommended, and this coincides with my own experience. There was a sandy area of about 80 acres which had been exhausted by growing rye and oats during many years without manuring, so as to be at last unable to produce anything but some sheep fescue and wild grasses. This tract was in fall lightly plowed, remaining during the winter in this state. Early in spring it was harrowed smoothly, whereupon matured pine-cones, collected during the latter part of the preceding winter, were at the rate of 5 bushels per acre evenly distributed over the field. When the heat in June had fully opened the cones, the field was dragged over with the brush-harrow, the dragging being only practised to shake the cones, and make them discharge those seeds which were still kept in the scales. The tract was then left undisturbed. During the next spring so many plants had come up, that this plot, by thinning, furnished sufficient seedlings to restock, for two years, some large openings in the adjoining woods.

One bushel of pine-cones weighs about 45 pounds, contains about 3,000 cones with 1 pound clean seed, or about 70,000 kernels.

Seeding Pines in open fields is often done broadcast with clean seed, using for the acre from four to five pounds. If Spruces are seeded, one pound per acre should be added. If winged seed is used, one quarter of the quantity just specified must be added. For the proper distribution of the seed, such sowing machines are commonly used as are employed in seeding clover. Should it be advisable to mix Pine seed with Spruce and Larch, one pound of the Spruce and Larch is substituted for half a pound of Pine.

Mostly, however, large tracts are seeded by drilling in the Pine seeds by which operation one-third part of the seed required in broadcast sowing will be saved.

As for the time of seeding, it makes a difference whether cones or seeds are used. The former should be distributed early in spring, while the latter are sown when the temperature has become somewhat warmer.

The best way to cover the seeds of the cones is that which has been suggested heretofore, as only a light cover is required. Clean seeds are usually covered with a wooden harrow, the teeth of its front row only being permitted to operate, while the others are interwoven with small twigs or branches of willows. In light soils the seed should not be covered deeper than one quarter of an inch, while in heavy soils the cover should be even thinner.

(*b*) *Beds for the nut-bearing Trees, especially for Oak, Chestnut and Hickory Trees.*

The storing of acorns, chestnuts and hickory nuts during the winter being attended by many difficulties, on account of their being easily injured by frost, wet, dry and heating, fall seeding can only be recommended, and this mode is always successful, if the mice be kept from the seed. Poisoned wheat or corn in drain-pipes has proved most useful. On the thoroughly worked and well prepared seed-beds, four drills about 15 inches apart, and two inches deep for acorns and chestnuts, and three inches deep for walnuts and hickory nuts, are opened with the hand hoe, and healthy, well selected acorns or nuts placed in the rows so close that they nearly touch each other, whereupon the drills are raked perfectly even with the soil of the bed. It is not necessary to fill the rows with ashes or burnt sods, or with compost; but where the means permit this application, it will be found of great advantage in the development of the plants. The beds are then covered with dry leaves, two inches high, and burdened with brush-wood to prevent uncovering by winds. When spring opens with warm days, the leaf-cover is removed and piled alongside the beds. After the plants have sprung up the ground should be cleansed and thoroughly raked. The leaves have then to be scattered between the drills, to be used as a mulch for preventing the growth of weeds.

The one-year-old plants may be transplanted to their place of destination (groves), if game is not apt to damage them there. Commonly, however, they have to be transplanted to the nursery, and raised to a height of from five to six feet to prevent game from eating the tops. This point will be mentioned again further on; here we only remark that if (what we prefer) two-year plants be used for the start in the nurseries, the seed-beds, during the second year, should be carefully cleaned, and the soil between the drills kept loosened.

Seeding large tracts of wood-lands with acorns is often done because the transplanting of oaks, on account of their large tap-roots, is not always successful. Some species, as for instance, *Quercus Ilex* or *sempervirens*, are only propagated by placing the acorns into the holes where the trees are to remain, because they form already in the first year a tap-root three feet in length.

In general, the seeding of large tracts with nuts or acorns is done in the following manner:

1. On soil which is not too heavy throw broadcast the seeds (about 8 bushels to the acre) over the unplowed field,* either harrowing or plowing under the kernels. On such fields sometimes furrows, three feet distant, are opened (from three to four inches apart) in which the acorns or nuts are laid, and covered three inches deep with the loose soil taken from the top of the furrow ridge. Four bushels of seed will be required for this operation.

2. Mostly the lands to be seeded down with nut-bearing forest trees, especially when the ground consists of heavy loam, should be well plowed and harrowed, where-

---

* Under favorable circumstances acorns will sprout and thrive even if very little or no pains at all is taken for their growth. Mr. Wm. Pickhardt, of New York, who owns about 24,000 acres of burnt-over woodlands near Schroon Lake, in the Adirondacks, some years ago, in March, sowed upon the snow three tons of white pine seed, and one hundred bushels of acorns of the German oak. He succeeded so well that the oak seedlings, one year after planting, measured from two to three inches.

upon in distances of about three feet, furrows about 4 inches deep are opened with a small plow, and the acorns or nuts placed therein, from three to 4 inches apart. This culture requires about four bushels of seed to the acre. Still less seed is needed when it is put in with a drill, the teeth of which should run from 3 to 4 inches deep. Make the rows three feet distant, and deposit the seed from three to four inches apart. In this case there are only from 2 to 2¹/₂ bushels consumed.

In regard to the number of bushels of seed used in seeding large tracts, due regard should be given to the size of the kernels, the above named number of bushels being calculated only for the largest acorns or nuts. When using smaller sized nuts or acorns, the said quantity of seeds should be decreased proportionately. As for the proper depth to cover the seeds of nut-bearing trees, the quality of the soil plays an important part in it. In a close, heavy soil a thinner covering is required than in a light, gravely or sandy. While a depth of from 2 to 3 inches is quite sufficient to make the seeds germinate in the former, it will do them good, if covered in the latter, as deep as from 4 to 5 inches; and this depth is usually resorted to when the seeds are sown broadcast over an uncultivated field with light soil, and plowed under.

(*c*) *Beds for Beeches.*

The seed-beds for the Beech tree are treated precisely like the foregoing, except that the leaves' cover remains unremoved for a longer time, to prevent too early a germination of the seed, the young plants being very susceptible to frost. Besides, these plants require much protection, at least for the first year, against excess of air and sun-light. It is, therefore, advisable to locate them so as to shelter the young plants against the south side. If this cannot be done, then pine boughs should be driven in suitable intervals into the beds, although the cleansing and loosening of the soil will be made tedious by it.

As it is less difficult to store beech-nuts for the winter than other nuts, seeding in spring gives often good results. But we prefer fall seeding, having thus obtained more vigorous plants.

Well-managed Beech forests are never permitted to become denuded, but are rejuvenated by preserving so many large trees as are required to drop sufficient seed nuts, and to cover the soil, thus furnishing to the self-sown seedlings the much needed protection against sun and air, up to the time when they can get along without further protection.

Seeding beech nuts successfully on a large scale requires not only the proper soil—good loamy soil, somewhat calcareous—but also a most thorough cultivation of the grounds to the depth of from 10 to 12 inches. The nuts are broadcast seeded over the unharrowed field, using from 3 to 4 bushels per acre, and thereupon harrowed in about one inch deep on heavy, and from 2 to 3 inches deep on lighter soil. Usually, however, seeding is done in drills from 3 to 4 feet apart, using one-half of the quantity of seed employed in broadcast seeding. Sometimes the nuts are planted in holes made at intervals of 3 feet. The rows are from 3 to 4 feet apart. For this operation only half a bushel of nuts is required.

The usual time of seeding is in spring, when cold weather is over, and no late frosts are expected, as the young plants, which will come up in about three weeks, are very tender, and liable to be killed by late frosts, unless well protected.

(*d*) *Seed-beds for Ashes.*

The seeds of Ashes ripen very late in autumn, and therefore are often left on the trees until the next spring, when seed twigs may be cut with hedge shears. The seed gathered in fall should be air-dried, and during the winter stored in the barn. If it be not practicable to dry them satisfactorily, they should be mixed with dry, sandy soil, and laid in small heaps on a place which is protected against rain and frost. To prevent them from heating, the heaps should be turned over during the winter several times.

In spring the seeds are freed from the sand by sifting. They are then so closely distributed in the drills of the well prepared bed that the winged seed kernels lap one over the other. The drill-rows are one inch deep and two inches wide. After carefully covering the seeds about half an inch, the beds are raked and overspread four inches high with moss, heath, straw or leaves, on the top of which should be laid brushes or twigs to keep this light cover in position, and to prevent the growing of weeds. In this condition the beds remain till next spring when the cover is removed, whereupon the plants appear above the ground. As these seeds mostly require a longer rest before they germinate, it is advisable, in order to avoid damage by mice upon the seed-bed, and damage by overgrowing with weeds in the field culture, to properly store the seed till fall time, and sow them at that time.

Weeding and loosening the soil between the drills, and slightly covering the root-crowns of the young seedlings is here, as in all seed-beds, a necessary requirement.

Ashes, Elms and Maples, which in forest economy are considered closely allied, are seldom found as pure stock, because they lose, in the middle of their life term, their soil-shading quality, allow the impoverishment of the soil, and the springing up of valueless bushes and trees. But if mixed together in seeding large tracts, good results may be anticipated. For an acre there would be required for each kind, if sown separately, pure cleaned seed, viz.: for Ashes, about 50 pounds; Maples, 30 pounds; and Elms, 25 pounds. If mixed together one-third part of each of these quantities of seed should be used to seed an acre broadcast, and only one-sixth part if seeded in drill-rows. The covering should be light and should not exceed half an inch; to effect this the brush harrow, or the reversed wooden harrow is employed to cover the seed.

(e) *Seed-beds for Maples.*

Although some varieties of the Maple tribe can be propagated by shoots, layers and cuttings, they are principally increased by seeding. The seed of most varieties ripens in spring or early summer, and should then at once be sown in well prepared beds. Only the *acer pseudo platanus* arrives at maturity in October. Its seed soon loses the power of germinating, and should be used in the same fall; but if it is necessary to keep it over winter, the air-dried seed should be put in bags, fastened to the beams of the barn in a place where no frost penetrates. Mixing the seed thus with dry sand, and then placing it where it will not freeze, preserves the vitality of the seed.

When sown in fall, precautions should be made against ravages by moles and mice—animals that are very fond of these seeds. In selecting the seed attention should be paid to its condition. When the wings begin to turn brown and the cotyledons are green and succulent, the seed is all right; but when the green color has disappeared, the kernels will not sprout.

Maple seed is sown in the same manner as Ash, viz.: very close, because the seed-wings take up much room. But no cover of moss, leaves, or bushes is required, as the plants, when sown in autumn, come up early in spring, and are not susceptible to frosts.

These seed-beds would always give the best result if the mice did not destroy the seedlings in the second winter by gnawing the young bark. This is difficult to prevent unless the mice can be exterminated before winter sets in, for the most damage is done during the winter, under cover of snow.

If sown in spring the seed sprouts in from four to five weeks, with the exception of *acer campestre*, which does not make its appearance before the second year. The seed, when sown in spring, should not be covered more than half an inch, and the ground should be shaded with leaves or straw to prevent the growth of weeds.

The bushel of air-dried Maple seed weighs about 15 pounds. If it should be determined upon to seed an acre broadcast with Maples, two bushels, or about 30 pounds of seed would be required, and for drill-seed about one-half of this quantity. But for reasons given above it will come seldom to this. The cover of broadcast sown seed must be light, and should not be thicker than one-half of an inch.

(*f*) *Seed-beds for Elms.*

The seeds are ripe in June, and can be kept, with care, till next spring; but it is better to sow them at once. For this purpose the beds are in time prepared, and the drill-rows (made in the same manner as for evergreen seed-beds) entirely filled with seed, and thereupon lightly covered, at most one half of an inch, with prepared loose humus soil or compost. The beds being apt at that season soon to become dry, it is necessary to water them in the evenings, and to use a cover of straw or heaths until the plants spring up. Usually this occurs from six to eight days after sowing, but it may be retarded by the season from two to three weeks.

Elms produce a great many infertile seed pods. Before sowing them they should be examined by a touch of the fingers, and by this manipulation should be ascertained whether the seed pods in the center of the round wings are full or empty. According to the proportion of empty seed pods, the seed should be used more or less freely. It is not advisable to obtain this seed from dealers, as it will seldom germinate. The grown up trees yield always plenty of seed, and this can be easily gathered by those who want it.

If broadcast seeding in seed-beds be resorted to, there will be required for the square rod one-quarter of a pound good seed. This is covered by sifting over it a layer of good compost, one-half of an inch thick.

Broadcast seeding on a larger scale would require 5 bushels, or about 15 pounds per acre; while drilling in rows with the proper distance (3 feet) could be done with one-half of the quantity of seed named.

(*g*) *Seed-beds for Alder-trees and Birches.*

Although the Birch and Alder-tree do not rank very high among forest trees, they are valuable in the economy of wood-lands, as they often thrive in localities where no other forest tree would grow, thus preserving the much desired soil-humidity and preventing soil exhaustion by surface evaporation. They belong to the same order—*Betulaceæ*—but differ entirely in their habits and requirements as to soil and situation.

The Alder is mostly found in wet and swampy grounds, whereas most varieties of the Birch are satisfied with poor, dry and gravely soil, and are not influenced either by the chemical properties of the soil or the nature of the lay.

The *Seed-beds* for Birches and Alder-trees are treated exactly like those for Elms, with the exception that their seeds do not like a very loose soil, and therefore the beds should be rolled down a little before distributing the seed. Seeds ripen from midsummer till October, and should be sown immediately after gathering when the catkins are still wet; the plants appear then early in spring. The Alder seedlings being very tender and liable to be destroyed by frost, should be covered by some leaves and twigs. Birch seedlings are hardy, and require no protection; but the proper sowing time for both is spring, and broadcast sowing is mostly employed. The seed should be very lightly covered with a wooden rake. If sowing in drills is preferred, the seed is sown in broad beds in the manner of the coniferous trees, and the beds are kept free of weeds till the plants have sprung up. They require careful cleaning and frequent watering during the first year. In the second year they reach already a height of from 8 to 10 inches in suitable soil—loose and rich in vegetable mould—and are able to be transplanted. But if they shall be used to fill out vacant spaces in the woods, or to form coppice-wood, three-year-old plants should be selected.

It is also advisable to gather these seeds rather than to obtain them from seedsmen, and for the same reason as above mentioned. The cones, or catkins, are picked in fall when their color has turned into brown, and before frost appears. They should then be air-dried, put in bags and hung up in a barn. In spring they will be found to have mostly opened and dropped the seed. Should the deliverance of the seed not have been fully accomplished, the cones have to be taken into a warmed room, where they soon will discharge the rest of the seed. Some collect the seeds by thrashing in fall the air-dried catkins in the bags, and store the cleaned seed in a dry barn in small piles protected against very cold and wet air, while some cut in the fall the twigs on which the cones grow, hang them during the winter up in the barn, and thrash them in spring. At all events there should be used for seeding only fresh seed, as the germinating power of most of the varieties lasts not longer than one year.

Birches and Alder-trees copse very well, and are in this way especially regenerated wherever this is practicable and advisable. This is principally the case with the Alder-tree, as it grows in from twenty to thirty years to a pretty large tree. The Birches do not grow so quickly, but attain later a very respectable circumference.

Seeding on a large scale gives, especially with Birches, almost always good results.* The soil, which usually will be of a light kind, should not be loosened too much, and the seed only slightly covered with the brush-harrow. For broadcast seeding there are required from 20 to 30 pounds per acre. Seeding in drills is seldom employed, but should it be determined upon, one-third of the seed used in broadcast seeding at least is spared. Birches are especially serviceable for the protection of Oaks when cultivated on a large scale. In such cases 10

---

* This I can recommend from my own experience. I recall an instance where a large tract of cleared wood-land with poor, gravely soil had been cultivated with crops for several years, and was then laid to rest. Soon it became covered with coarse grasses and small bushes. At the end of one summer this tract was burnt over and prepared for spring seeding. Next spring oats were sown and properly plowed in and harrowed. Some days later cleansed birch seed, about 15 pounds to the acre, was sown broadcast over the oats, and lightly covered with the brush-harrow. The result was surprisingly successful. The birch seedlings, coming up much later than the oats, were, during the summer, protected against the sun and kept back, so that at harvest-time the young plants were not hurt by the cradle. After the removal of the oats from the field, the birch seedlings received a new start, and entered well prepared into the winter season. Seedlings were so numerous that two years later a great many plants were taken up, and used for setting out a copplce plantation. The expense of the whole operation was fully covered by a rich oats crop.

pounds of Birch seed are used and sown over the ground, after the acorns have been properly planted.

The arboreous vegetation in American forests contains many varieties which cannot be considered as forest trees proper, and yet are of great value either to serve as soil cover, nurses, or to fill in between the main crops, or to promote the growth of the principal forest trees in any other wise. To these belong the Poplars, Willows, Basswood, Locust, Catalpa, Tulip tree (variety of the Magnolias) and Hornbeam. The propagation of these trees offers no difficulties ; catalogues of our seed dealers give satisfactory information in regard to that point. But the great value the Hornbeam has, both as copse-wood and as an intermixture with other forest trees, may justify a few remarks in regard to its propagation. The seed contained in hop-like catkins ripen in the fall. A bushel of winged seed contains from 6 to 7 pounds of clean seed. The catkins should, after being gathered, be spread out and dried in the shade until the seed can be thrashed in bags. As the seeds do not keep long, it is advisable to sow them at once, or at latest next spring, after having preserved them during the winter in the same way in which Ash seeds are preserved. Thus preserved the seed may be kept till the second spring. The seed should be covered very slightly, one-quarter of an inch. It is best to use only fully cleaned seed. Of these, for broadcast seeding, are used from 22 to 24 pounds per acre ; for seeding in drills, 12 to 16 pounds.

An essential requirement for every seed-bed of forest trees is the selection of good wood-land soil, the best that can be found, but rather mild loamy than heavy clayey soil ; for seedlings grown on good soil are much better than those grown on poor grounds. They have more and better roots, and are in a better condition to endure the shock sustained in transplanting, and to grow in their new locality. But the soil should not be made rich by manuring, as this produces a rank growth, which prevents the proper ripening of the wood. All that is required is a ground sufficient to make a healthy tree.

The place to be selected should have a situation well protected against cold and drying winds; and yet this location should not be such as to enfeeble the seedlings and render them unable to go through the hardships of young forest trees. If nurseries for forest trees are to be established upon the open ridges of a mountainous country, the proper protection may be obtained either by fences, or, if permanently established, by surrounding them with earth walls from 6 to 8 feet high, on the top of which are planted Birches, Pines and Alders.

CHAPTER XV.

PLANTING FOREST TREES.

The planting of forest trees can only succeed in places where there is no grass, and where no grass would ordinarily grow for some years to come. In such places, especially in poor sandy or peaty soil, two-year-old plants without ball are usually selected for planting; assigning, of course, to the proper soil, the suitable kind of trees—to the poorest soil the Pine and Birch. But Spruce should always be intermixed even on the poorest ground. The Spruce can be made to grow upon such soil by means of abundant watering. Even a slow growth of these trees is satisfactory, as they have only to serve as nurses, and to form the undergrowth of the pine forest.

The mode of planting is as follows: ashes from dried peat-sods, or compost having been prepared the summer or fall preceding the planting season, as soon as the frost is out of the ground, and the latter warmed to some extent, the seedlings are taken from the seed-bed by a spade; the earth and the plants carefully separated with the fingers so as not to injure the roots and fibres. Thereupon lots of from 10 to 12 plants are placed together, crowns of roots exactly upon crowns, and tap-roots shortened to the length of from 6 to 8 inches. The plants, piled up in a basket in which they have to be well moistened and protected against the rays of the sun, are then taken to the planting ground. Here everything should have been in time prepared for their reception. Planting holes of about six square inches are cleared with the hoe in distances never exceeding one yard. On ground which is covered by moss, the latter is simply removed.

On clay soil the holes should be made in the preceding fall, and should be about 10 inches square, and from 7 to 8 inches deep; the earth dug out of the holes should be placed alongside. In the spring, shortly before planting begins, the holes are filled up, the top soil going to the bottom, and the surface completely leveled.

A pail of brine is prepared principally of clay and water, mixed with ashes or rich humus soil and a little salt. This mixture should have such consistency that the plant roots, dipped into it, retain a thin covering, but never so much as to paste the roots and fibres together. This can easily be ascertained by trial. From 10 to 20 plants are at a time dipped into the brine so as to coat the roots preparatory to planting.

The planter carries a basket with thoroughly worked compost, peat ashes or good humus soil, upon which the coated plants are deposited, and a short-handled axe. The latter is driven up to the handle into the center of the prepared and leveled spot, pressed to both sides and then carefully taken out. With the left hand two plants are lowered in the cleft to a point just above the crown of the roots, one finger separating the plants, and while thus suspended a handful of compost is with the right hand sifted into the cleft between the plants. The axe is then driven in about one inch distance from the cleft and pressed a little toward it, so as to cover the roots with earth. The second cleft should then be filled up with a few light strokes of the axe.

On stony soil it would be impossible, or at least very difficult, to operate in the manner just explained. In such soil use should be made of a steel-pointed iron planter, by which a square hole is driven into the ground, large enough to set two plants in the manner just described.

Watering the plants after setting is very well, if it is done carefully with a rose sprinkler, and lumping of the soil is avoided ; but generally it is not necessary, except in times of impending drought. If watering during the hot season has to be resorted to, it should be done late in the afternoon or evenings.

It will not do to set one or two-year-old plants on grass lands or on such soil as is favorable to the growth of grass and weeds. On such ground plants from four to six years old should be set, as these are able to resist the encroachments of grass and weeds. Where game may do damage, deciduous trees of such height should be planted as to prevent the animals from touching and eating the top shoots of the young trees. To raise trees of that size, *tree nurseries* are necessary. These should be located at or near the places to be planted, so that the considerable risk and expense of transporting larger trees, and to acclimatize the young trees to the natural conditions of their future habitat may not be unnecessarily increased. The ground for these nurseries should be plowed and subsoiled in fall to a depth of from fifteen to eighteen inches, and exposed to the action of the air, rain and frost during the winter. At the proper time in the following spring the nursery ground should be harrowed, then plowed and again harrowed, and then the one or two-year-old plants are set in the proper one of the two following ways:

(1) NURSERY LINES FOR CONIFEROUS TREES.

Beds are laid out of the same size as seed-beds, at most six feet wide, in order to permit from four to five rows of plants to be set from five to seven inches apart. The rows are marked by a cord or chain, and the planting is done by the short handled axe, as just described, after the plants have been previously dipped into the clay mixture. In these beds it is desirable to set but one good plant to the hole. Watering immediately after planting is necessary; but it should not be done close to the plant, but at the *second* cleft.

Careful cleaning and stirring the soil is a matter of course. But the two operations should never be continued late in the summer, as they encourage the tree growth too late in the season, and the wood thus made does not ripen well, but will be killed by a strong winter frost; they should be entirely omitted the latter half of the summer previous to the transplanting of the young trees, in order that *a strong ball* may be secured, and the taking out of the trees with balls in the following spring facililated.

(2) NURSERY LINES FOR DECIDUOUS TREES.

The first thing to be determined upon before laying out these nursery lines, is the decision of the question whether we intend to raise only small trees, of from three to five feet height, or larger ones—up to twelve feet. In the first case the plants are set from ten to twelve inches apart in the rows; in the other case from eighteen to twenty-four inches. But even for the latter purpose it is advisable to plant first closely (say ten inches apart), and transplant later further apart at another place in the nursery. Although we would not advise that a tree be transplanted in the nursery more often than is absolutely necessary to attain the purposes aimed at, repeated transplanting, if carefully done, promotes the development of the root system, as each planting will require a little trimming of the roots, and by shortening of the tap-roots, which too often run deeper than is desirable, the growth of the lateral roots will be favored—this being the most desirable point in the culture of whatever tree may be in question. If the transplanting in the nursery is not done with the proper care, and the roots, owing to their injured condition, have to be pruned heavily, no vigorous growth can be expected, but debilitation is induced and a premature death must be expected. The mode of planting the one or two-year-old plants is the same as with the coniferous trees; but the holes opened with the axe must be correspondingly larger for the greater root development of the two-year-old plants. It is, therefore, a better plan that such plants as have a strongly developed root system be transplanted into the nursery lines *when one year old.*

In transplanting young trees of from four to five feet high in the nursery, for the purpose of raising larger ones of from ten to twelve feet high, the axe of course will not answer. In that case holes of sufficient size should be dug with the spade and hoe, and the lateral roots should be well bedded in by hand in their original position. Many deciduous trees, especially oaks, incline much to forkiness, which tendency should be promptly and carefully suppressed in the nursery by proper trimming, unless it is intended to raise such forky trees on account of their usefulness in certain manufactures, as ship-building, etc. But in general the forester should always have the knife ready to clip the inferior limb as soon as forks appear. Sometimes the superior limb has to be trimmed off, if by the growing of the inferior a more desirable standard tree is formed. In such cases no certain rule can be given, except not to allow the tops of the trees to go into forklike shapes.

PLANTING WITH THE BALL.

When coniferous trees previously transplanted into the nuresry rows have reached an age of from four to six years, they are ready for final transplating and have to be taken up with the ball—that is, without disturbing the roots or removing the earth from them. In this condition they should be put in holes large enough to give ample room for the ball. The taking up is done by the spade, a little ditch being dug along the first row of the plants, and the plants cut out in square blocks. The plants with the balls are carried on barrows or carts and deposited near the plant holes. Before setting in, the planter must examine carefully the depth and width of the hole, as the roots must have the same position and the same level relative to the earth's surface in their new place as they had in their old one. Therefore, if the holes are found to be too deep, some earth is thrown in; if too shallow, they are dug deeper. The tree is then set perpendicularly in the center of the hole, and the space around the ball filled in with loose soil, and gently pressed down with the feet.

It is true, close planting does well for quickly covering the ground. But as this is an expensive operation, owing to the number of young trees to be planted, and the subsequent labor of thinning them out, it is usually better to maintain a greater distance. The rows are then laid out five feet apart, and the trees in each row three feet from each other.

Diciduous trees can be transplanted more easily without ball, especially when they have been already transplanted, and thereby acquired a better developed root-system.

PLANTING WITHOUT BALL.

The larger deciduous trees of from six to twelve feet in height are always transplanted without ball. It is, however, advisable to manage the transplanting so as to retain some of the old soil between the rootlets and fibres. The holes are dug according to the extent of the roots, so that they may have room in width and depth, without changing in the form they have grown.

On heavy soil the holes should be opened in the fall, if spring planting is intended, in order that the winter frost may assist in breaking up the soil mechanically. At planting time the young trees, unless they have been taken up in fall and safely heeled in during the winter, are taken out of the nursery, injured roots and such as extend too deep (especially the taproots) being trimmed off, the clay brine already mentioned is used, and the trees brought to the holes. Holding the tree with the left hand perpendicularly, the forest planter, using a hoe in his right hand, fills the spaces between the roots with loose humus soil. If horizontal roots are bent down in this process, they should be raised up, and supported with earth so as to keep their natural position. For such trees as have root systems which incline to lateral extension (Spruces, Beeches, etc.), a little mound of earth should be made at the bottom of the plant-hole, upon which the tree is set, so that the roots spread out in a natural way. Special attention must be given that the roots are perfectly imbedded in the soil without leaving cavities, and that the original position of the fibres be maintained. The fertile top soil dug from the plant-hole should always be used to fill the bottom of the pit to feed the roots and fibres, while the raw soil taken from the bottom serves for leveling the surface. Planting is finished by gently pressing down the earth around the tree with the feet, and covering the recently disturbed soil with sods or stones, leaving uncovered a space of a few inches in diameter around the base of the tree. The sodding will keep the dirt in the plant-hole fresh and moist.

In cases where dryness or looseness of the soil renders plant growth at the start uncertain, especially for planting the hardy kinds of Pines upon sterile lime-stone soils and shifting sands, the report of the Department of Agriculture for 1887 recommends the "puddling in," and describes this method as follows: "A thin puddle is "made of two parts water and one part loamy forest soil "or mold. In planting, a conical hole is made to re-"ceive the plant, and while holding the plant in the "hole, the puddle is poured into it with a cup. The "puddle must be stiff enough to hold the plant at a pro-"per height; yet not too thick, because in such cases "it would not fill the bottom of the hole, but would ad-"here to the sides, and thus the tips of the roots would "have no covering, and would die off. To be sure, in "hot weather the upper loamy layer dries out quickly "and hardens; but this layer, not being hygroscopic, "prevents the drying out of the lower strata, which is "the important point to secure in the quickly drying "sand. The cost of this method of planting is about "double that of ordinary planting in holes."

Sometimes it is desirable to plant trees upon loose, boggy ground, where plant-holes, if made in the usual way, would always be full of water, thereby killing the trees set in them. In such cases trees may be planted entirely above the surface ground by spreading out the roots, and throwing dry, good soil over them. The conical mound thus formed is then covered with inverted sods or soil taken from the vicinity, and the tree, if of larger size, is fastened to the ground for some time by wires running from the trunk of the tree to pegs in the ground. By this method we are able to plant trees in places where the impossibility of obtaining drainage would entirely prevent planting in the usual way. Trees with taproots, of course, cannot be used for such plantations, as the condition of the underlying soil does not favor the roots penetrating deeply into the ground.

The transplanting of seedlings or saplings from the woods, if this be carefully done, should meet with the same success as if they were removed from the nursery. Usually, however, the loss in transplanting saplings grown naturally in the woods, is much greater than with nursery-grown seedlings, because the forest planter seldom gives to the young trees all the opportunities for their growth which are afforded to them by the soil and the surroundings in their habitat. To transplant spontaneously grown seedlings of the shade-enduring kind (Beeches, Spruces, Hornbeams), is much more difficult than to transplant seedlings of the light-needing kinds (Pines, Oaks). With the latter it does not make much difference whether they are grown in the woods or in the nursery, whereas the former will only succeed if the conditions of their habitats are fully provided for. But if this is possible, and the removal is done carefully, there is no doubt that a dense spontaneous growth of saplings in one part of a forest can be very serviceable in restocking other denuded parts of the forest. However, in order to be certain of success in this matter, saplings taken from the thick woods should first be transplanted into nursery lines, to give them an opportunity to get acclimatized and to obtain, by the help of air and light, a greater development of the branches and twigs, which in the thick woods usually are suppressed at the expense of the formation of the trunk.

The general rules in regard to trimming of roots and tops hold true also for the transplanting of seedlings taken from the woods. Experts in this matter, however, contend that these seedlings should be pruned more severely than those from the nursery.

In conclusion some remarks in regard to tree planting in general may still be added.

1. Great care must be taken to protect the seedlings against the rays of the sun and drying winds. Planting, therefore, should be done only in mild weather, when no strong winds prevail, and the sun is not too powerful. If possible, the operation should be performed during a gentle rain. If this be not practicable, and if we have to work in warm, sunny weather, there should be no more plants taken up from the nursery than can be planted within the next hour; for if the young trees are exposed to wind and light, the roots and fibres often shrivel up, and become unable to furnish food to the tree. Should it be impossible to observe this direction on account of the distance the trees have to be transported, while being removed they should be coated with the clay brine, and be well wrapped in wet moss or other damp materials, to check loss of moisture through foliage and roots. Trees which appear to have suffered from evaporation of moisture during the removal, after their arrival should be heeled in—that is, laid in trenches,—and if they have suffered much, they should for some time be entirely covered with fresh soil until taken to the place where they are to be planted.

2. The best time for transplanting trees is during the dormant period, when the sap in the tree does not run. This period lies between the end of autumn and the beginning of spring. Conifers, however, may, with the exception of the Larch, be transplanted even after budding. Under favorable conditions, planting may be done either in fall or spring with the same good result;

but in cold climates like ours, spring planting is to be preferred, as only at that time new roots are formed, through which the tree can obtain the sap necessary for the support of the top growth. In such a case the trees to be transplanted should be taken up in fall, and heeled in, till planting time in spring arrives. This treatment facilitates spring planting very much.

3. All trees should be planted a little higher above the ground than they previously stood; * at least they should never be set deeper. In this respect the place from which they are taken makes no difference, be it the nursery or the woods. It is often the case that workmen without experience do the planting, and not making the proper allowance for the looseness of the soil, set trees too deep into the hole. This treatment kills a great many trees during the second year after transplanting and more often prevents their luxuriant growth. But if trees are planted a little higher out of the ground than they previoulsy stood, they develop a better and quicker growth, have a longer life time, and will give better timber of an even texture.

All top trimming or shortening of the main branches should be avoided, even with deciduous trees, except when, in taking up, the roots are much bruised or broken, and, therefore, have to be shortened in order to obtain smooth ends of the roots and fibres. In such a case the top has to be cut back so far as to restore the proportion in which crown and root system were prior to the removal. Transplanting causes a great disturbance in the life of a plant, arresting the cir-

---

* The only exception to this rule is the planting of *one-year-old Pine seedlings* in very poor soil. In such ground the seedling should be buried so deep that only its top shows above the soil. How F. B. Hough, in his "Elements of Forestry," on page 55, arrives at the conclusion that "as a rule trees in transplanting should be set deeper than they stood before," is more than we can comprehend, as experts in this matter agree in accepting the reverse to be true.

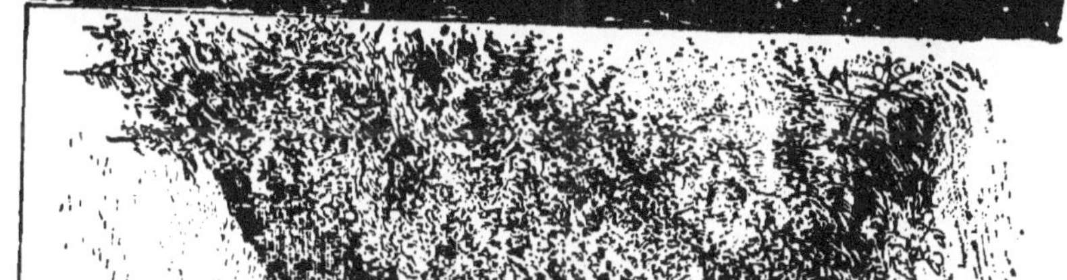

culation of the sap that is constantly going on under the bark of the tree. To overcome this shock, and to make a new start, the full activity of the leaves and roots is put in requisition, as the plant takes up a part of its food by the roots, and assimilates it by the leaves. But how can this be done when an operation has been performed by which both organs are made to suffer so greatly as to be unable to discharge their ordinary functions.

As for the rest, the forester, in transplanting, should look into and examine closely the principles by which nature is working, furnishing to the plants everything which they require for the full development of their inborn recuperative power. It is true, the use of the short-handled axe in planting trees does not seem to correspond with this advice, as the side roots are thereby somewhat pressed together; but this is only recommended with very young seedlings, and especially with young Pines and Oaks, as they have long taproots, the conservation of which is of chief importance during the first years of their growth. Moreover, as the soil in the plant-hole is very loose, the side roots of the saplings soon succeed in vindicating their right of spreading sideways.

TRANSPLANTING LARGE TREES.

The forester is sometimes called upon to move large trees from the position in which they have grown for years to another. This work is often required on mountain forests, and in such cases as are called "Forest Gardening", and which have been alluded to on page 62. It necessarily involves some amount of anxiety to the operator; it is the most precarious and uncertain operation in regard to its result, the forest planter has to perform. Success can only be attained by the most careful execution of the work in every detail.

The preparation of the trees beforehand is undoubtedly

the most important of the details in connection with the work. No large tree that has stood a few or more years in one position undisturbed should be transplanted without being prepared some time beforehand by operating on its roots. The growth of trees should be checked skillfully by a system of root-pruning. The customary way of doing this is to dig a trench around the tree, at such a distance from the stem as may appear desirable or necessary to secure a requisite breadth of roots all around to support the tree when it is finally transplanted. The trench is dug deeply enough to get to the nethermost roots. Usually all the roots are cut away, and the trench is again filled in with good rich soil. This is commonly done twelve months before the transplanting is to take place, and the objects are to administer a check to the tree and induce a free production of fibrous roots.

No doubt these objects are, in the main, successfully attained in most cases, but in such a way as to minimise the chances of success when the final operation of removal is performed twelve months hence. It is no uncommon thing to find the entire circle of soft fibrous roots that may have been formed during the intervening growing season fall away when the trench is again opened for the purpose of removal. If this occurs, and it is hardly pospossible to prevent it more or less, the tree is then more seriously crippled than it would have been had it been lifted at the time of preparation. A much better method is to open a trench twelve months beforehand, a considerable distance from the trunk, to such a depth as will reach the lowest roots, and work gradually in towards the center in a regular way all round, laying bare every root, preserving the smaller and fibrous roots, and cutting away the stronger ones until within a foot or two of the stem, when the trench should be filled in, laying the preserved roots out carefully, and covering them with good fresh soil. When treated in this way, a greater proportion of the fibrous roots can be preserved at the final lifting. These fibrous roots are those on which ultimate success depends, and every means should be taken to preserve as many of them as possible. The tree may require to be stayed or supported during the time intervening between the period of preparing and that of removal. If the top is a heavy one, and the position exposed, it should certainly be secured against disturbance.

The *removal* must be done with great care. It is the critical and anxious part of the work. The seasonable time must be regulated by the character of the tree. If it is deciduous, very early spring is preferable to late in our climate. In warmer climates, however, early autumn it the best time for the removal, when the fall of the leaves has not yet taken place. The tree will, owing to the disturbance in the preparation of the preceding year, have made no luxuriant growth, and such growth as it may have made will ripen early; there is, therefore, no danger in an early removal, and every other consideration is in favor of it. If the tree is Evergreen, the operation of final removal should not be performed till late spring. Immediately after the first symptoms of returning activity are observed, is the proper time for the removal of Evergreen trees of all kinds.

The work of removal involves the consideration of the apparatus required, and this depends on the size of the tree to be operated upon, and the distance it has to be carried to its new position. There are various machines invented for the purpose of removing very large trees, but they are costly concerns, which are not needed in the every day routine of the forester's work. For trees of ordinary size there exists no necessity for anything so costly or cumbrous as any of these machines. A cart or wagon of any sort will do the work of transporting the tree quite well, provided care is taken to prevent all avoidable injury either to the stem or the roots in loading or unloading it.

The most important point is the lifting of the tree in such a manner as to minimise injury to the roots. The operation should be conducted in the same way as that of preparing, already described. Begin by opening a trench at the same point as was opened for preparing, and work in a circle round the tree. After the trench is opened use forks only and use them with great caution among the roots to prevent their destruction. Clear away the earth loosened by the fork with spade or shovel, so as to keep the trench clear, and prevent the roots being covered or entangled with it till a solid ball is reached a little way from the stem all round. It is desirable to keep this ball of earth and roots intact, and at this point the fibrous roots liberated from the soil in excavating should be tied up in bundles and laid conveniently over the ball. What remains to be done, in order to liberate the tree, is to excavate under the ball all round, so that it may be drawn by ropes attached to its top to one side or the other. The ball is then to be bound firmly up in mats, secured in such a way as that it may be safely transported any reasonable distance without breaking to pieces.

When taken to its new position, the pit in which it is to be planted should be examined to ascertain that it is quite large enough to allow of the roots being spread out straight. There should be no doubling of them back to accomodate them. Badly injured portions should be cut away with a sharp knife, as they are spread out, and the finest of the soil sprinkled over them. Let there be no treading in of the soil, but use water copiously instead. Water will fill in all hollows and cavities in the soil in a more perfect manner than treading, and also leave the soil in a thoroughly genial condition for the roots. A mulch of straw, litter or leaves placed over the area occupied by the roots, a day or two after planting is finished, will be beneficial. The tree must be carefully secured against disturbance by wind. The most effectual way to do so is by strands of rope stretched from the top to pegs in the ground.

In conclusion it may not be amiss to add some directions for transplanting large trees, which were given in a pamphlet published by the Department of the Interior in 1885 for the celebration of Arbor Day. There it reads as follows :

At the outset it is necessary to bear in mind that the tree is a living body, and that the process of removal interferes with its functions, and when it is displaced from the ground, causing an arrest of the circulation that is constantly going on between the tree and the soil, a severe shock is sustained. Every root-fiber and its spongiole destroyed lessens by so much the chances of success, and when a greater portion of these are gone, the tree is forced to depend on its own vitality to supply a new set of rootlets before growth can take place.

In the beginning bear in mind that it is important not to injure the roots and to preserve as many as possible, particularly the small ones, for these are what must be depended on to start the growth in the new life. Where trees are dug up to be removed a short distance, preserve all the roots if possible.

When the tree is out of the ground, exposure to the sun or drying winds will cause evaporation, which is very detrimental to the tree, and is a common cause of failure, and one which is often overlooked. If, however, the tree has become shriveled and dried, vitality may often be restored by burying the whole for a few days in moist soil ; but it is far better not to have them get in condition to need any such remedy, which at best cannot restore the tree to its original condition.

In excavating holes for planting, it is necessary to dig

very deep, unless for a tree with a tap-root ; it may even be hurtful in a hard soil by affording a place to hold water under a tree to its injury. The roots of young trees grow near the surface, and the holes should be large enough to allow the roots to be extended their full length without cramping or bending.

In case it is very dry at the time of planting, it is a good plan to puddle (see page 97) the soil around the roots, always covering with dry earth. In this way moisture will be retained for a long time. Avoid too deep planting. The roots must not be placed beyond the action of the air ; about the depth they were in before removed, or a very little deeper. (We would say " higher," instead of deeper. See the remarks on page 100, sub. 3.) When filling, press the earth from the first firmly, so as to leave no spaces, and have it compact about the roots. This latter point cannot be too thoroughly attended to, and, of course, to do this well, the soil must be finely pulverized and no lumps be allowed in the filling. It will be necessary to use the hand to place the soil in spaces where the spade cannot go.

The time of setting is best when the soil has settled in the Spring and become warm, so that trees not being removed begin to start. Earlier than this is not so well, for the sooner the tree begins to grow after being set, the more likely to do well. We believe the proper time is the Spring, the best time for planting all kinds of trees, although early Fall planting is often recommended. Evergreens often succeed well planted in August ; still we would rather risk them in the Spring, just as they are ready to grow. Evergreens are the most sensitive of any to drying while being removed, and if once allowed to become dry it is all-day with them ; no amount of pains or trouble can restore the lost vitality. For this reason they can be removed but short distances, unless very carefully packed.

As more or less of the roots are removed or injured, it is necessary to prune the top when transplanted. This has generally been done by cutting all the branches back; but a better way is to remove a portion of the branches, leaving those strong ones that are in position to give the tree a well-shaped top. If all the branches are left, and the proportion between the tops and roots balanced by cutting all back, in after-growth some of these branches will require to be removed—an injury, perhaps, to the tree. This certainly will apply to fruit trees. Sometimes trees for ornament or shade require to be cut back to make a thicker top or one more symmetrical.

Large trees are removed in Winter with a large ball of earth attached to the root, and, though a heavy job, it is the only* successful method of doing it. A trenchcan be dug at the proper distance around the tree, and filled with coarse litter previous to freezing, and also the holes to receive the trees, which will much facilitate the labor.

Small trees do better than large ones, and it is better to be to the trouble of taking care of them one or two years longer than to have them grow too long in the nursery row. Trees grown on good soil are better than from poor soil. They have more and better roots, and are in better condition to grow in their new location. Of course, it is not desirable that the soil where they have grown should be so rich as to produce such a growth that the wood will not properly ripen, but sufficient to make a strong, healthy tree. A tree in poor soil has weak, spindling, feeble branches, and, like a starved animal, takes a long time to recover, even when placed in better soil with better feeding.

After large trees are properly transplanted, they should be staked, to prevent swaying around by the wind. When the ground is soft, the movement of the top

* This is a little too much claimed.

creates a displacement of the roots before they have taken any hold in the soil, resulting in injury or death to the tree. Mulching must not be dispensed with. Its object is to keep the soil moist until the roots obtain a strong hold. This may be overdone. Mulch for shade only. A large mass of decaying matter is more hurtful than beneficial. We can not avoid all risks in transplanting; but if these conditions, which we repeat, are followed, the risk will be very much lessened: (1) Careful removal; (2) protection from drying while out of the ground; (3) setting in warm, well-pulverized soil; (4) hard tramping* the soil about the roots; (5) judicious pruning; (6) stalking; and (7) mulching.

All this requires care and labor; but it will make the difference between a thrifty tree, and a stunted, unhealthy specimen.

---

* We would not advise hard tramping, but rather gently pressing down—not too firmly—to the level of the surrounding surface. At all events, heaping the soil around the tree should be avoided.

CHAPTER XVI.

THE CARE OF YOUNG PLANTATIONS.

1. *Protection afforded by the older trees to young and growing ones:*

Young forest-trees are very susceptible to many external influences, as, for instance: frost, aridity, extreme sunshine, excessive growth of grasses and weeds, etc. In the natural reproduction of forests we are able to protect the saplings and seedlings during the trying years of their first growth by retaining a proportionate number of the larger trees, which, in due time, and with the growing up of the young trees, are gradually cut down, till, at last, nothing but the younger trees remain.

We may also employ the same means in the artificial reproduction of forests, either by growing first a hardy kind of trees, under the protection of which, at the time of the first thinning, ten or fifteen years later, the more tender species, intended for the future stock of trees, may be planted; or, by sowing or planting both kinds of trees together, selecting for the protecting trees those varieties that are fast growers, thus enabling them to afford shelter to the more slowly growing tender ones.

Upon denuded woodlands, especially upon such as are surrounded by natural forests, hardier and quick growing trees, as, for instance, poplars, birches, willows and even pines very often spring up by themselves. In such cases, we have only to plant the better and more tender kinds mixed with the hardier saplings, and we may expect an undisturbed, continuous growth of the tender trees under the shelter of the hardier ones.

Even bushes and shrubs may be made to serve as nurses for young trees. They have the advantage of being the cheapest means for reaching the purpose aimed at. But no return of wood material is realized when they have to be removed later on, while timber obtained from the hardier protecting forest-trees pays at least the expense of cutting, and, sometimes, even the cost of planting.

For nurses to the young, shade-enduring trees, such kind of trees are usually selected as cause only a light shade. So, for instance, the principal species of the firs, as *Abies pectinata, A. nobilis,* and, upon good soil, the spruce may be advantageously grown in the shade of the common pi e or birch ; the beech, which is quite as difficult to grow as *Abies pectinata* or *picea,* can be grown in the shade of the poplar, willow, alder, etc. If the nurses are properly selected they will grow quickly without preventing the development of the future stock of trees, but their own value increases with the length of time they remain. These nurses, belonging mostly to the light-needing varieties, afford still another advantage to the protected trees, as they have the tendency to crowd out such trees of their own kind as grow up too thickly, and to drop off, for want of light and air, their own lower branches, furnishing thus to the protected shade-enduring trees every condition to mature and attain a sound development.

2. *Cleaning and Thinning.*

We are able to obtain great advantages both in natural and artificial plantations by applying a proper system of cleaning and thinning.

Cleaning.—As soon as the nurses threaten to overwhelm with too much shade the protected young trees, of which we have been speaking, they have to be cut down so far as to prevent them from interfering with the luxuriant growth of the future and predominant stock of trees.

In the natural reproduction of forests, the quick growing sprouts from stumps become often very troublesome, because they are apt to subdue valuable, young trees that have grown up from seeds, and which are mostly slow growers. In such case, the sprouts of each stock should be very much reduced in numbers, and only a few strong ones should be left. In the course of time, the latter will again increase and begin to do harm to the neighboring self-sown seedlings of the more valuable kind. Then the sprouts are still reduced, and but one for each stock is kept over. This will be removed when the saplings have reached such a size that they will not be in any danger from subsequent sprouts of the felled tree.

Thinning.—It is an undeniable fact that in natural forests sometimes over one hundred thousand young trees can be found growing upon an area of one acre; and yet we cannot expect to raise more than from one to two hundred full grown trees upon that space. Left to itself, the natural forest will eliminate in the course of their growth all those trees that cannot stand the struggle for existence; and, finally, there will be only some giants found upon each acre of woodland. This constant natural thinning-out is more prevalent during the earlier years of tree-growth than in their advanced age, while the remaining trees increase in strength and vitality. Then there commences a struggle which soon assumes such proportions as to involve danger to most of the survivors. Here the skilful hand of the forester is required to terminate the contest, especially when the trees are of the same age and equally developed. True, in such case, although a tree cannot expand laterally, it can attain a good height. However, this being a forced growth, the individuals become extremely weak and succumb in a body to such forces as high winds, great snow drifts, etc., or their accretions become from year to year smaller till the whole body falls a prey to insects or blight.

In a natural forest, where trees of different kinds and

ages grow up together, the conditions for natural thinning out are more favorable. Here, nature itself does the principal work of timely thinning out, and the elementary forces do—as is generally known—less damage in forests where conifers are intermixed with foliaged trees, than in forests of pure stock. And still the helping hand of the forester can do a great deal to produce a quicker development of the trees and to increase their strength and growth.

It is an old rule in forestry to commence thinning *early*, and repeat it *often*, but always to do the work *moderately*. But after the lapse of from 60 to 70 years, when the trees have attained their full height, it is expedient to open out the stock itself more freely, in order to give the trees a chance to extend their remaining branches, and thus enable them to accelerate their accretion of wood. The branches of trees in forests under sixty years of age should be allowed to grow pretty close together—so densely as not to show any gaps. Such forests will produce the best timber, as the trees then will develop branches only on the higher part of the trunk, leaving the lower part free, and yet keeping the soil well shaded.

Absolute rules as to the exact time for the periodical thinnings cannot be given, except that the soil should *always* be protected from light, sun and wind, and that the vigorous growth of those trees which are intended for future stock, should never be interfered with by their companions. Which trees should be selected in thinning out a forest, can best be shown in forests with a pure stock of trees, *i. e.*, with trees of the same kind and mostly of the same age. Here you find three different classes of trees, viz.:

(1) *The dominant*, which have grown ahead of the others.

(2) *The governed*, which, although lifting their crowns in the sunshine, are narrowed in by the other trees.

(3) *The subdued*, which are overgrown by both the preceding classes.

There is no doubt that the latter class should be taken out entirely, while the first should remain intact, excepting those trees which are infested with dangerous insects, or have incurable defects in the bark and trunk. In such cases, even dominant but faulty trees should be removed in time, to avoid spreading of evil, and to give the confined trees in their neighborhood the possibility of extending laterally and attaining a larger growth.

As to class 2, it makes a difference as to what kind of trees are growing in the forest. The light-needing species require a more open position, and, therefore, a stronger thinning; while the shade-enduring thrive even when they are so closely grown that sunlight cannot fall upon the lower branches of the trunk, and, therefore, require but a moderate thinning.

The *location* has great influence upon the extent to which the thinning out is to be carried. Upon good, fertile soil the gaps and openings made by a more extensive thinning will fill up soon, even if there be a northern or northwestern exposure. But on poor soil, even a small interruption of the density of the tree-growth is apt to cause drying up of the soil, springing up of weeds, blowing away of the leaves on the ground—all these being conditions detrimental to tree-growth, and which should be strictly avoided. For this reason the wood-material obtained by thinning out forests upon poor soil, and, which usually is removed at once, is often not taken away, but is left on the spot to fall a prey to the destroying effect of the elements, thus enriching the soil by the decay of twigs and leaves.

As to what *age* the trees should attain before the forest is thinned out, we must remember that the younger trees have a tendency to grow upward rather than to extend laterally. They, therefore, can stand a much greater density than older ones, and do not need to be so carefully thinned out as the older ones. At all events the margin of woods should be left thicker, not only in respect to tree-growth, but also in regard to the undergrowth, formed by shrubs and brushes, which have sprung up there. For only in this natural way can the noxious influences of the sun, light, and drying winds upon the forest-growth at the margins of the woods be obviated. The same rule holds good if there are openings in the interior of woods on account of the interruption of the density of the trees in those places. The point never to be lost sight of in the management of forests is, to keep the soil fully shaded, especially when it is poor and dry.

In woods of mixed growth, such as occur in naturally grown forests, thinning is done on different principles. There the light-needing trees grow ahead of the shade-enduring ones, and seemingly subdue them. Nevertheless, the latter must not be removed, as they form the most important part of the forest, and thrive even in the shade of the light-needing trees. In thinning such forests we have to consider both classes of trees separately, and by looking at the overgrown trees, we have to remove of this class (light needing), those which prevent the full development of their companions; while looking at the undergrowth we have to remove of the shade-enduring class, such as are subdued or are likely to be subdued by trees of their own class. However, to proceed here correctly is not an easy task, and should never be left to the discretion of ordinary workingmen.

Old trees growing among young stock should not be felled in the ordinary way, but gradually removed by first separating the branches so as not to injure the young trees surrounding them; and then the trunk after being felled, should be cut up and carried piece by piece, with the least damage possible to the after-growing trees.

3. *Removal of large branches.*

The removal of the large branches of trees, which have been retained and left to increase in growth, is seldom needed in the management of forests, as in properly kept forests the density of the trees forces them to follow the light and sun, and grow up in height, thereby keeping back the branches, which, by the increasing shade from the tops of the young trees, gradually drop off. In this way the trunks of trees in the high forests become clear of knots and attain the form so valuable in lumber and timber. Wherever large branches appear on forest trees a defective position of the trunks has been the cause. To remove such branches will seldom be worth while, except in very valuable trunks the value of which may sometimes be increased by the removal; and when room is wanted to enable young trees, growing in the shade of larger ones, to increase in growth. The removal of such branches becomes necessary when in so-called middle forests trees are left overgrown to attain a greater height. In such a forest each of these large trees grows up more or less separated, pushes out its branches laterally, and when not properly attended to, forms less [useful] wood in trunk and stem, and more in the useless branches. Moreover, these branches have a damaging effect upon the sprouts of the cut stock growing under them by shadowing and preventing their vigorous growth; and for this reason they frequently have to be removed.

In removing a large branch from a tree, we must first endeavor to minimize as much as possible the extent of the wound; especially we must avoid causing a split in the bark remaining on the tree. In order to attain this we should not cut the branch in one cut, but make first an incision underneath, about twelve inches beyond the place where the branch is to be cut off, then saw entirely through the branch about one inch further outward, and thus the largest part of it is removed. Thereupon remove the remaining stump by sawing at a right angle where it joins the tree, but never in a line running parallel with the standing tree. [See illustration.]

If there be more than one branch to be removed from a tree, commence with the highest branches, at the same time taking off the dry ones. If the trunk retains its branches for one third part of its entire height it is sufficient for its vigorous growth.

A, first incision ; B, first cut ; C D, second cut, correctly executed; C E, incorrectly made cut.

The most favorable time for removing large branches is late in the fall and in the first part of the winter, because the healing of the wound will be completed when the sap begins to run. The sap is then prevented from running out of the cut and causing it to rot. No painting with tar, oil, paint, or the like, is required.

4. *Undergrowth as a protection to the forest-soil.*

It is generally conceded that a favorable condition of a forest is only practicable when the soil is constantly protected against the drying influences of sun, light and wind. For this reason the skillful forester always endeavors to keep the soil in forests of foliaged trees covered with tree-leaves, and in coniferous forests covered with needles. The growth of grasses, moss, heaths, bushes, etc., should be stopped wherever they appear in forests, and precautions should be taken to prevent their return. Such vegetation appears in the openings of imperfect and neglected forests, and in those woods that consist of light-needing trees, when the foliage of the trees becomes too thin to overshadow the soil. Up to within a short time it was customary to plant these openings and gaps with shade-enduring trees, viz., foliaged forests with oaks, beeches, maples and hornbeams; and light-needing coniferous forests of pines and larches with spruces and firs, by which measure the grasses, weeds, etc., would be killed off, while the newly planted trees under the shade of the old stock would grow luxuriantly, thereby increasing the wood production of the forest. All this sounds very plausible, but experiments made in Germany at different experimental stations during several decades show that trees planted for the protection of the denuded soil use up most of the plant-food in the surface soil, and thereby damage or at least keep back the growth of the old stock of trees. It may be that this observation will not coincide with similar experiments yet to be made in this country, because our natural forests contain much more plant-food than the artificial forests in the old world ; but, even in Germany, intelligent foresters insist upon preserving whatever is produced in the woods that will cover the soil and retain its humidity, thus preventing undue exhaustion by surface evaporation.

CHAPTER XVII.

PROTECTION OF FORESTS AGAINST ANIMALS AND ELEMENTARY FORCES.

The doctrine of the protection of forests includes all subjects and events by which forests and forest-products may be imperilled, and the measures to be taken in order to obviate and lessen the severity of such evils. These protective measures are directed either against animals, or elementary forces.

I.—THE RELATION OF THE ANIMAL KINGDOM TO FORESTS.

There exist many animals which are useful and promote the well-being of forests, others whose value is doubtful, being at some seasons and times beneficial and at others injurious—and still another class whose presence is always detrimental to forestal growth. In the second case—doubtful animals—the injury inflicted is often overestimated and war waged against animals which, although doing little harm, are persecuted because their habits are unknown, and, therefore, a prejudice prevails against them.

A.—*The Useful Animals.*

Among the mammals we find some carnivorous animals which feed principally on noxious insects, (bugs, caterpillars, pupas, butterflies and their eggs) viz.: bats, some species of the shrew-mouses, moles, hedgehogs, or porcupines and skunks.

The burrowing habit of the mole is sometimes injurious in forest-nurseries, but in the ordinary forests it is of great advantage, as it loosens the ground and renders it more adapted for the reception and retention of humidity and fertilizing matter.

Martens, some species of the weasel, the fox, polecat and badger, are very useful also. These animals feeding *principally* upon mice, and many noxious insects, should be allowed to remain. Special care should be taken to spare the young of these animals as they live *exclusively* on mice and insects.

The importance of birds, as valuable factors in forests is very great. With the exception of some of the larger ones as for instance: the eagle, vulture, falcon, the hawk, the horn-owl and the raven, most of them contribute to the healthy growth of trees. The smaller birds are always hunting the enemies of tree-growth, and their multiplication should be encouraged in every conceivable way. They, therefore, should not only be spared, but also protected against their principal foes, cats and squirrels, during breeding-time. The starlings, woodpeckers, all kinds of thrushes, black birds, whip-poor-wils, the purple martin, the oriole, the cedar-bird, the cat-bird, the red-eyed vireo and the like have proved especially beneficial; they feed not only upon insects, but in winter, when the ground is covered with snow, some of them search industriously for the eggs of the insects buried in the bark and twigs of the trees. No gunner should shoot one of these little animals of the feathered tribe.

Singing birds live without exception on insects. The forester should devote to them special care, and set aside certain places where there are bushes or hollow trees, as these afford the most desirable opportunities for nest-building. In case such opportunities are lacking, breeding-boxes should be hung up in the trees in order to afford the feathered tribes the facilities to build nests and rear their young. It is advisable to leave wild fruit-trees as crab-apple, wild cherry, plum, pear etc., which usually are scattered over a forest area, undisturbed, as the fruit serves to support useful animals during the time that insects, caterpillars and eggs of insects cannot be had.

The various kinds of lizzards, most of the snakes, the blind worms, frogs and toads are also useful animals as they devour not only obnoxious insects, but many of them attack also rats, mice and other small rodents.

But even among the insects we find many which are carnivorous, and feed mainly upon the smaller and noxious kinds of their own tribe. To this class belong the following beetles:

(1.) The lion beetles *Calasoma calidum* and *Calasoma scrutator*, of which the former hunts mostly during the night, while the latter kills and eats all soft-bodied larvæ during the daytime.

(2.) The elongated ground beetle, *Pasimachus elongatus*, preys also upon all soft-bodied larvæ.

(3.) The *Cicindelidæ* are very appropriately named "Tiger-beetles." They live in burrows, and are continually at the top of their burrows waiting for insects which they catch and drag into their holes where they eat them at leisure.

(4.) The most widely known and justly appreciated beneficial beetles are the Lady-birds, *Coccinellidæ.* They perform the work of exterminating noxious insects quietly and silently, and devour countless numbers of their victims in a short time.

Beetles are not the only beneficial insects; a still larger number is found among the Hymenoptera. Special notice deserve:

(1.) The dragon-fly or adderbolt-fly (*Libellula*), ants and wasp-flies. The latter two are even in their larvæ state carnivorous, and prey upon other insects, devouring also their eggs.

(2.) The white faced hornets are busy all day long in

search of larvæ and slugs with which they feed their young.

(3.) Other insects prove beneficial by depositing their eggs in the pupas of injurious caterpillars upon which the young feed, when hatched. To this class (parasites) belong the ichneumon-flies (*tenthredo*) which range all the way from flies an inch in length to so minute species that they scarcely are visible to the naked eye. The larger kinds deposit only one egg in each victim, while some of the smaller leave their entire complement of eggs on one caterpillar. The eggs hatch soon, and the larvæ eat their way into the worm where they consume all the substance that would otherwise go to make the future noxious moth.

B.—*The Doubtful Animals.*

Mistakes are often made with regard to the good or bad offices of birds by those who ought to know which are their friends and which their foes. This holds especially good in reference to

The jay. It is true that this fellow in the spring hunts after the eggs of the smaller, useful birds, and sucks the meat out of them with great relish ; but in the fall he industriously collects ripe acorns and beechnuts, and buries them in various places in the ground, in order to lay aside food enough to supply his needs during the winter. Fortunately he forgets most of the hiding-places, and the result is that the seeds sprout and produce fine seedlings.

The sparrow, of which lately much complaint has been made, is in many respects detrimental to field and garden products, as he feeds principally upon fruit. But in the winter time he is very useful, living then upon eggs of the insects which he picks from the bark of the trees. During the breeding-time, in spring and early summer, he destroys a great many insects in order to satisfy the wants of his young that will take no other food for the first weeks of their life. An excess of their multiplication should be checked by the gun or trap. Either fried or boiled, for soup or stew, they make an excellent meal.

C.—*The Injurious Animals.*

Animals of prey such as bears, wolves, catamounts, wild-cats, etc., should be unmercifully persecuted and killed off as they devour the nobler kinds of game and also animals useful in promoting the forest-growth.

Of the mammals, the rodents are the most obnoxious animals, especially the *beaver*—one of them alone being able to cut down in one night a tree measuring 12 inches in diameter. In the State of New York they are now nearly exterminated, but their pernicious work can still be seen on streams and creeks in the Adirondack region on the so-called "beaver meadows." The beavers built their dams across the streams causing long back flows by which the surrounding trees and bushes were water killed or drowned in the ponds formed through the dams. These ponds became, in time, filled by the decaying wood material and other debris of the forests, and furnished the aquatic plants the soil in which they found not only root, but such rich plant food that the whole pond soon was overgrown with coarse grasses. After the extinction of the beaver the lumbermen have resumed this work of destroying trees by water. For in order to cheaply transport the logs through the Adirondacks, dams are now built, causing back flows that annually kill more trees than ever have been there destroyed by fire.

Mice are very obnoxious to forest-growth. They feed upon tree seed, gnaw off the tender bark of young trees, and bite entirely through small seedlings and saplings. Foliaged trees are the principal object of their ravages; but they do not spare conifers, especially when the forests are surrounded with fields upon which a rich grass-cover exists. They hide during the winter under the grass and direct from thence their feeding expeditions to the neighboring woods. It is, therefore, advisable to cut late in the fall the grass in and around young plantations as short as possible, thereby preventing the mice from making their headquarters near the young trees. But if the damage is done, the girdled trees should be cut early in spring clean above the ground, in order to invite a stump growth. True, girdled trees will also sprout, but as the sap is unable to circulate in the trees, their vitality is weakened to such a degree that they die off during the next season. If the mice increase so much as to become a plague there is no better means in which to fight them than to foster their natural enemies in the animal kingdom, and to often drive hogs and cattle into the endangered groves, thus disturbing them in their feeding-places. In fenced-in forest nurseries mice may be destroyed by putting poisoned grains in drain pipes; but to do the same in the forests is not advisable for the reason that useful animals would be killed when feeding upon the poisoned mice.

The squirrel, rabbit, rellmouse and some species of the dormouse are just as injurious as the mice; the first one besides gnawing the trees, consumes the eggs and young of small birds. Squirrels and rabbits should, therefore, be shot or trapped. The other named foes cannot be destroyed except by promoting the multiplication of their natural persecutors, as is recommended in regard to mice.

Game, especially deer, when too numerous, will do much harm to young plantations by feeding upon small seedlings, and rubbing their horns or branches against the taller ones. Ashes and spruces, grown up to the size of hop-poles are sought out by deer, and their bark is peeled off the stem as far up as the animals can reach.

In this way game can do much harm to young plantations. The forester must know how many heads of game a forest can support without imperilling the tree-growth; he should kill off the excess or cause it to be killed off. This is one of the many reasons why the learned forester should have the exclusive care of game in his territory. To entrust the duty of caring for the game to so-called "game keepers" as is done in our State, is preposterous, and serves only to cause collisions between officers who should be subjected to the directions of one and the same superior, and act harmoniously in the interest of the preservation of both game and woods.

The most careful attention should be given by the forester to the habits and life history of insects noxious to forest-trees, because, without a correct knowledge of those circumstances, he will not be able to stop or minimize the often enormous ravages accomplished by these small animals. Their habits are very manifold. Some make their appearance in February and March, others in summer, and still others in the fall. Some go during one year through all four stations of their development (egg, larva or caterpillar, chrysalis or pupa, butterfly beetle), others require several years for their complete evolution, the young of others are hatched several times in one season. It is also of interest to know in which state of development the insects attack the trees. Commonly the larvæ do all the harm by feeding upon leaves and twigs; sometimes the fullfledged insect, especially many beetles, perform this operation. To observe what kind of trees are particularly sought after by one or the other species of insects is also important. Some species confine themselves to one kind of trees, others attack several kinds; the most obnoxious are those which feed upon both coniferous and foliaged trees. Some insects consume only leaves, others feed upon the buds; some live inside the tree, others between tree and bark; some are always to be found but not numerous; others appear seldom, but when they appear, they muster up dangerously great numbers; some are slow in their movements and walk only; others fly and cover very quickly large stretches of forests.

From this it will be seen that a keen observation is required to be able to employ at the right time, and in the right place, the proper means to moderate the damages, and to prevent the further spreading of insect-pests. The most efficacious measure of obtaining these results consists in sparing and even fostering the multiplication of the natural enemies of the injurious insects. The equilibrium between useful and obnoxious animals is kept up in the animal kingdom by the production of such animals as persecute the injurious ones. This law is nowhere more obvious than with insects. There a considerable number can be looked upon by their destruction of obnoxious insects as real benefactors to mankind.

It is further recommended as a preventive means from insect ravages the removal of stumps, dry trees and branches, cut wood and timber, and the peeling off the bark from timber in case it cannot be shifted from the forest, whereby the breeding-places of insects are destroyed. The most effective means to suppress the insect-plague, especially in wild or natural forests, is the introduction of a systematic management, of which the first step would be a correct and periodically repeated thinning by which we in time obtain a thoroughly sound and vigorous growth of trees—and to such trees obnoxious insects cannot do much harm.

If the just mentioned means to *prevent* the spread of injurious insects are observed, it is not difficult to get rid of them completely. For this purpose the bark of trees invaded by insects should be stripped off and burnt, the dead trees should be cut, and unless removed, should be burnt up; all stumps, even those of pines, should be barked, and the bark be removed or burnt; for stumps, especially those of trees, which have been felled during the preceding two years, are a general resort for all kinds of destructive boring insects, and should be pulled up. But as this, if done on a large scale, is very expensive, we reach the same end by tearing off the bark, the naked stump being not frequented by obnoxious insects.

The forester, who has made careful observations on the habits of destructive forest insects, is further able to keep his district clean by putting at proper places, so-called "trap-trees." Healthy, living trees, especially conifers, are felled in many spots of the forest at the time when the obnoxious insects commence flying around, and left on the ground without peeling the bark or removing the branches. The insects like to deposit their eggs in these newly cut trees, and if such trees are removed or burnt up ere the eggs are hatched, all danger from attacks of the destroyed generations will be over. But the forester must endeavor to obtain correct knowledge of the habits of injurious insects, because without that it would not be possible for him to determine the most proper time for removing and destroying the "trap-trees."

The United States Entomological Commission, published in 1881 in its Bulletin No. VII a very interesting and useful treatise on the insects injurious to forest and shade trees, from which we can see how numerous and pernicious these insects are in this country. Those who want more information upon this subject, than the limited space of this publication permits to give, are referred to said pamphlet, the author of which is Dr. A.S. Packhard.

According to the said bulletin oaks are attacked by 214 different species of insects; elms by 43; hickories by 87 ; black-walnut by 11 ; butternut by 18 ; chestnut by 18 ; locust by 20 ; maple by 37 ; birch by 19 ; beech by 15 ; tulip-tree by 9 ; pines by 102 and spruces by 24.

Besides enumerating and describing those insects the bulletin also contains an account of the remedies to be applied in destroying them. But the average forester will seldom be able to make use of them, they being too expensive and causing too much labor in extensive forests. If large tracts in the forest are taken hold of by insects, we have to decide which parts can still be saved, and then apply every means to suppress the pest. But if it has spread to such a degree that human help cannot more be of any use, the afflicted trees have to be cut, and if possible to be disposed of as wood products, or, if that is not practicable, the torch has to be applied to them with proper precaution against spreading of the fire beyond the limits of the infested tract. After the fire has destroyed the insects, larvæ and eggs, the denuded area should be reforested at once, in order to close the opening made in the forest as soon as possible, and to prevent the elements from making inroads upon the opened forest.

In the same proportion as the species of forest-trees of this country greatly outnumber those of Europe the insects detrimental to them are here more numerous than in Europe. But the damaging influence of the insects here upon forest-growth has not been so generally injurious on account of the *diversity of trees* growing in our wild or natural woods, where insects may feed undisturbed upon certain trees preferred by them ; and for the *extensivity* of our forests, where the damages of the several species of insects may be not so remarkable on the single trees ; both circumstances furnishing at the same time very good opportunities for creating in large numbers the natural persecutors of obnoxious insects. However, we should not be careless in this matter as not only in our

Adirondack forests,* but also in other States,† serious complaints are being made that valuable tracts of timber are dying off. We must watch closely the working of these little animals, and neglect nothing that can contribute to their suppression. This duty should be considered by us the more urgent as in regard to the *extensivity* of our forests close observers have already pointed out the next future as the time where complaints of wood scarcity ‡ might be more justified than boasts of superabundance; and then, of course, the great *diversity* of trees will have gone also.

II.—INJURIOUS INFLUENCE OF THE ELEMENTS UPON FOREST-GROWTH.

A.—*Frost.*

FROST causes injury to forest-trees in various ways: sometimes the cold during the winter is so excessive that entire groves of our hardiest trees are killed. This occurs principally in *valleys* where there are great stretches of marshy or swampy land, and also in adjacent higher land looking towards the south. Not unfrequently the

---

* Cfr. Ann. Report St. Forest Commission for 1885, pp. 52, 59; Report for 1886, p. 14; Report for 1888, p. 27.

† A West Virginia paper lately had the following item:

MORGANTOWN, West Va., Sept. 14.—During the present Summer large tracts of valuable black spruce timber along the valley of the Cheat River have died, entailing a loss of tens of thousands of dollars upon the owners of the land. Botanist C. F. Millspaugh and Entomologist A. D. Hopkins of the State University have undertaken to investigate the matter, in the hope of being able to point out a remedy. It is suspected that some insect is at the bottom of the disease which is attacking the trees.

‡ The *Lewiston* (Me.) *Journal* of April 4, 1890, contained as follows: "It's rather queer—the fact that the Boston and Maine had to suspend operations on its Kittery-Portsmouth bridge for a whole season because the company could not find suitable timber for its completion. The depletion of our forest treasures is no myth.

frost causes fissures to appear in the bark and wood of trees, by which they are weakened to such a degree that they succumb as soon as the weather becomes very cold. During early spring, when the running of the sap in the trees has commenced, and a very cold spell follows after some warm days, the sap often freezes, especially at the south-side of the trunk; then the bark, covering the frozen sap, becomes loosened, thereby exposing the underlying wood, which in consequence goes to rot.

To prevent these casualties there is only one means, viz.: the preservation of the close density of the forest, especially at its margin where it borders on an open field or a very young plantation. This means of prevention may in case of need be assisted by cultivating "*wood-mantels.*" A wood-mantel is a strip of ground along the margin of a forest upon which hardy trees are planted at such distances that the single trees may be able to send their roots both perpendicularly and horizontally into the ground so as to fully resist the fury of the wind-storms and to develop, far down upon the trunk, strong branches by which cold winds are prevented from entering the forest.

Alternate freezing and thawing of the surface soil causes often the greatest injury to young plantations, especially when they are produced by *seeding*. In such case the roots are lifted and separated from their hold upon the soil. The deep roots which penetrate below the reach of frosts are broken off, and from the higher roots the earth is more or less loosened; finally, the plant is lifted by the expansion of the surface soil, and the remaining roots are laid bare. The seedling then dies. The only protection against this evil is to allow the natural grasses and weeds to extend moderately over the ground of the plantation so as to furnish a covering for the plants not unlike that afforded by snow. In forest-nurseries where, under no circumstance, grasses and weeds are allowed to grow, we can prevent the damaging influence of frost upon the plants by covering the rows with a layer of evergreen boughs.

The late frosts in spring when the trees have already developed their buds are the most injurious, killing young trees completely and affecting the older ones so far as to incapacitate them from producing seeds and from making any accretion in wood. This evil appears most frequently in wet or swampy valleys, where the evaporation of moisture prevents the access of the warmth contained in the upper layers of the atmosphere, and thereby increases the cold developed by evaporation in the soil. In such cases drainage should be applied to let off the excess of water; but when this is not practicable, hardy trees should be planted for the protection of the young ones, and retained till the latter have reached a size large enough to overshade the ground and to prevent too strong an evaporation of the moisture in the soil. Pines, hornbeams, alders and the American aspen are best adapted for this purpose, and even large bushes may be advantageously used.

In the swampy parts of mountainous regions there occur, sometimes, late in summer heavy though not lasting frosts, which may do a great deal of harm insomuch as after such a spell a second growth of wood takes place, which will not ripen by the time the winter sets in, and is then killed by frost. Oaks and beeches are especially subject to this casualty The best one can do in such case is to plant spruces which stand these vicissitudes very well.

Sun heat does damage to forests when there is a want of a proper water supply. If this can be procured all danger to the trees is over. Irrigation will seldom be practicable. But a great deal of the natural moisture can be retained in forests by preserving a compact density of the tree-growth, and keeping the soil well shaded by heavy foliaged trees. Should the management of the forest require giving the trees some more light in order to increase the accretion of wood, the *complete* clearing by a total felling should not longer be postponed than is unavoidably necessary, as in the open space the augmented falling of dew will benefit a young plantation more than if the seedlings are grown beneath *isolated single* trees; under which they are apt, owing to the reflected rays of the sun to be burnt and to dry up. In regions where the sun is known to injure tree-growth, Scotch pine (*pinus sylvestris*) should be cultivated exclusively. As is well-known, this tree grows where other kinds are regularly burnt up; but as soon as the pines commence to show openings there may be planted among them other and more valuable kinds of trees which, unprotected, would not stand long continued sun heat.

The *winds* produce evil effects by desiccating the soil and blowing away the fallen leaves which cover the ground. Both troubles can be avoided, or at least lessened, by retaining the fullest possible density of the tree-growth, especially at the margins of the woods. Should this not be practicable the establishment of so-called "*wood-mantels*" as described on page 129 is advised. The fallen leaves being better retained at the ground when there is a small growth of grasses, it may be sometimes advantageous to open the forest a little more, causing thereby the growth of a thin grass layer upon the bare forest-soil. At any rate, wide openings in the woods should never be allowed; but if the same by any accident occur, planting of hardy trees and the intermixture of conifers with foliaged trees should be undertaken at once, omitting the removal of the stumps of felled trees.

Excessive rains are apt to do much damage to forests, especially to the various cultures which, in a properly conducted forest-management, will invariably have to be undertaken. Planted seedlings cannot be much injured by rain; but the rows in which the seeds are distributed may easily be washed out if they are very long and not laid quite horizontally. For this reason it is recommended to interrupt long seed-rows often, and never neglect to give them a horizontal and level situation.

Inundations within the forests, caused by long continued rains may also do much injury by washing away the precious uppersoil consisting of rotten and half rotten leaves of the trees and twigs; and by hurting tree-growth itself through temporary submersion of the roots and parts of the trunks; but most of the damage is done where forests abut for long distances on streams which are apt to overflow, especially at the opening of spring when the ice-covering is broken up. In such case big floating ice-cakes are sent by the current into the woods exposed to the river-floods, cutting or bending down every tree which is not strong enough to withstand the pressure caused by the intruding ice-cakes. In order to prevent or at least to lessen those dangerous actions of inundations, copse-wood, with short periods of rotation should be cultivated on the forest territory as far as it is exposed to such overflows. The copse culture is here recommended because the trees, best adapted for it are quick growers, reaching soon above the high water mark and possess in their elastic stems and branches efficient means to break the force of currents, thereby lessening the dangers threatened by the floating ice-cakes.

The banks of such streams should be planted with rows of so-called "Pollards"* to ward off, as much as

---

* Pollards (in German *Kopfhölzer*) are hardy but well copsing trees of which not only the tops but also parts of their trunks are lopped off so that about 8 or 10 feet of the stems remain. At the new top sprouts will come out forming new branches. By this treatment we obtain more powerful trees which are able to resist the inroads of the ice-cakes and to detain them from entering the over-flooded parts of the forest.

can be done, the big rampant ice-cakes from entering the overflown copse-wood and destroying its tree-growth.

Heavy snowfalls do much more harm than rain to forest trees, especially to the conifers, as most of them retain during the winter a thick growth of leaves which form a substantial bed for the snow. But in mountain regions snow falls sometimes in October or November when the deciduous trees have not yet thrown off their foliage, and then these trees are also liable to be hurt by snow.

Snow acts most perniciously when falling in large flakes upon the branches of the trees while they are frozen on the outside. The flakes then accumulate upon the branches and twigs in such quantities that the tops of the trees form a nearly unbroken mass of ice, which weighs down the trees and sometimes destroys entire groves. The most approved safeguard against this occurrence consists of (1) a properly made thinning, together with a somewhat wider planting than is usual in plantations, and (2) the dividing up of the forest, *without interfering with its compactness,* into smaller tracts, separated by avenues or paths from 10 to 12 feet wide, laid out, if possible, so that the principal rain and snowstorms strike the paths crosswise and not in the direction of their length. See page 60, note. In restocking denuded woodlands planting is also for the same reason to be preferred to seeding as in the latter case an overcrowded condition of the seedlings can seldom be avoided. This is particularly true when pines and spruces are reproduced by seeding.

Woods in which conifers grow mixed with foliaged trees are less exposed to damages by snowdrifts, because they do not present an even surface, but one which is interrupted at the places where the defoliated trees stand. The snow settles then all around the naked deciduous trees without hurting them, and is in a great part prevented from settling upon the surface stretching over the tops of the conifers.

Damages caused to forests by an excess of humidity in the soil, which has to be drained, and by drifting sands of adjoining sandlayers are not infrequent. We shall treat of them at the proper places in Part II and III.

Fire is the most pernicious agent in the destruction of our forests. It is seldom that such fires can be traced to incendiarism. They mostly result from the carelessness of lumbermen, tourists and their guides. True, the establishment of the State Forest Commission, in 1885, has done much to prevent fires, and the principle that protection is better than cure has proved also in this case to be the best guard against fire. But often fires originate in the woods without human agency. Lightning has been the most frequent cause of wood-fires, although in some cases they may have originated from other causes as for instance from the spontaneous combustion due to the decomposition of pyrites, which is known to have set fire to beds of lignite in the Saskatchewan region.*

It is, therefore, very necessary that besides precautionary measures stringent rules regarding the extinguishing of fires occurring in forests and denuded woodlands should be adopted. The establishment of a proper road-system, and the division of a large forest into districts and plots separated by paths and avenues contributes much to confining forest-fires. Commonly they originate upon light, dry soils, when overgrown with conifers and covered with a thick layer of resinous needles; while a disaster of this kind hardly is ever known in forests with heavy clay or loamy soil upon which foliaged trees grow.† A discarded cigar or a blown out pipe bowl

---

* See American For. Congress 1888, page 50.

† Therefore in Germany, where railways pass through coniferous forests, and it is feared that the sparks flying from the locomotives may

INDIAN FACE AUSABLE POND. MT. COLVIN.

thrown upon forest soil of the former sort readily communicates fire to its surroundings. The smouldering sparks eat through the dry vegetable mould, attack the scant grasses and mosses and make so much headway that the green leaves of the young conifers are soon invaded. The least breeze will fan the smouldering mass into flames which spread rapidly to the tops of the larger trees, and are then beyond control.

Happy if you discover the fire when it is still confined to the inflammable material on the surface soil. All that is necessary then is to have some energetic men with rakes, brooms and shovels to rake the grasses, leaves and other ignitible substances, scattered over the forest soil, several yards ahead of the fire *towards* the burning mass, so that all litter and other combustible material in front of the fire is accumulated into a wall. It will not be difficult with a sufficient force of men to put out with their shovels and spades the approaching flames and confine them to the raked-up wall.

Much more difficult is the task of stopping a forest-fire after it has reached the branches of the larger trees and is running up to the tree-tops. Unless a heavy rain sets in the only means for putting the fire out is to make, at a proper distance ahead of the invading fire, a broad passage in such manner that the trees standing there are felled and thrown towards the advancing fire. As this work takes much time while forest-fires make quick headway, the opening in front of the fire should be begun at such a distance from the fire that the felling is finished before the flames reach the margin. Otherwise the

---

light the accumulated leaves and other ignitible material, as dry heather, mosses *a. s. f.*, it is customary to guard against this danger by *safety-strips*, formed by not-coniferous trees that are planted along the line of railways, as for instance birches, oaks, poplars, etc. Besides the ground of these strips is always kept clean of dry leaves, litter and other combustible material.

entire labor is frustrated, and the work has to be done over again, at a greater distance from the fire, thus sacrificing a still larger part of the forest than would have been destroyed if the distance was at the first properly taken. As soon as the fire reaches the row of felled trees a sufficient number of men with shovels, spades and wet brooms should be in readiness to work, and to use every means to extinguish the sparks and flames which fall upon the overturned trees.

Although the methods employed by the management of European forests in preventing the spreading of forest-fires are at present not yet fully available in our State, it may not be amiss to briefly describe the mode of European warfare against fires. This mode is in general as follows :

"Whenever a forest-fire is discovered the church-bells in all neighboring villages begin to ring and all able-bodied persons—men, women and children—turn out with axes, spades, shovels, rakes, brooms, etc., under the guidance of acknowledged leaders. They combine their movements, according to the direction of the wind and other circumstances, and dispose their forces with intelligence and promptitude. A mode often resorted to is the *contre feu*, fighting the fire with fire just as in the Prairies is often done. Knowing the forest well, they direct their forces to one of the *safety-strips*, (*i. e.* open paths in the woods upon which no shrubs or trees are allowed to grow) or to the most favorable spot on the path of the fire. At a sufficient distance ahead of it, an extended line of workers wider than the fire is formed and set to work to remove as much of the inflammable material as possible. They cut down and burn and trample and shovel earth and carry away stuff, etc., and when the fire in its course reaches that spot, it finds little food, hesitates, and at last is generally conquered."

Our forests are not always surrounded by villages, the

alarm bells cannot muster crowds of willing workers to our distant wildernesses; therefore, we cannot yet act in case of emergency as they do in Europe. But if we cannot extinguish the fire in quite the same way as they do, we can do just as much to prevent it, and to limit its ravages. The best means adopted in Europe for preventing the spreading of the fire over a large extent of the ground, is the laying out of their forests, and dividing them in somewhat isolated independent blocks by means of the *safety-strips*, in German called "*Schneissen.*" * With such openings you can much more easily subdue an approaching forest-fire than if the work of extinguishing has to be commenced in the midst of an unbroken forest.

However, forest-fires, especially in coniferous woods, cause another injury much beyond the actual destruction of timber by burning, in this, that the trees that have been killed or even scorched by the fire become principally liable to attacks by wood-boring insects. The larvæ of these by boring large galleries in the substance of the wood, will in a single season render it worthless for sawing or use in any other form than, as fire wood and quite inferior for that. It is, therefore, the best we can do with a burnt over wood plot to utilize the remains as soon as possible for charcoals.

---

*See page 60, note.

CHAPTER XVIII.

THE TRANSFORMATION OF THE WILD OR NATURAL WOODS INTO CULTIVATED FORESTS—WHAT THE AMERICAN FORESTER SHOULD DO NEXT.

WHILE the calling of the European forester chiefly consists of establishing and caring for artificial forests—originated either by seeding or planting—the destination of the American forester points to the transformation of our still abundant, but very much abused natural or wild woods into cultivated forests. In a properly managed forest there are from three to four times more *useful* trees than in a natural wood. The duty of the American forester, therefore, is to apply his ingenuity and experience *to make a certain area of woods, without disturbing their permanency and their economic influence,* producing from three to four times more than it does now.

It is true that exact knowledge of scientific forestry, as applied in Europe, may help him to understand how most easily to effect this transformation; but as the main principles, upon which scientific forestry is based, are no strangers to our intelligent agriculturists and arboriculturists, there is no doubt that we can readily find persons fully qualified for a *beginning,* and that they will be followed by others who will endeavor to acquire the full knowledge of the theory and practice of this science, completing what their predecessors may have left unfinished, or correcting such defects in the treatment of woods as close observation and experience has shown them to be erroneous. Up to the present time, there has been no demand for skilled foresters in this country. Nay, the framers of our Forestry Act of May 15, 1885, prohibit in §8 with the words "the forest preserve shall be forever kept as wild forest lands" the application of any system of forest management by which the rich products of an area, containing nearly one million acres of woodland, may be utilized. Our Forest commissioners, therefore, can hardly be blamed when they construed their duty to preserve the State forests only as a direction to secure the forests from the ax of the lumberman, and from the torch of the careless or wilful incendiary. *

During the last few years, however, when it became more and more apparent that our State forests, under the present laws and management, could not be preserved, but that their deforestation was progressing to such a degree that the watersheds of our principal rivers were imperilled, a large number of the most prominent men in the city and State of New York commenced a movement which culminated last year in the formation of the Adirondack Park Association for the purpose of greatly enlarging the territory of our State woodlands, and preserving the forests more efficiently by advocating the application of a systematic management of the woods.

This is a very timely movement which undoubtedly will make a lasting mark upon the history of the political economy of our State. As just before mentioned, we possess among our citizens many who are both theoretically and practically well acquainted with all matters pertaining to the growth and reproduction of forest-trees, and with the exploitation of woodlands. Such men, if endowed with good executive ability and assisted by experienced civil engineers, could be safely entrusted with the introduction of a systematic management of our State forests. Generally speaking, their efforts would be directed:

(*a*) To insure the permanency of tree-growth.

(*b*) To develop and increase, after a well-considered

---

* See Report of the St. For. Com. for 1888, p. VI.

plan of thinning, pruning and felling, the productive capacity of the forests, and

(*c*) To restock the denuded woodlands by seeding or planting such trees as are most desired and best adapted to soil, climate and location.

In particular, the labors to be performed during the first four or five years would consist of the following:

(1) A surveyor accompanied by an expert on soils and woods should first survey the whole tract, and then, under the advice of the expert, mark off and map out such subdivisions as are indicated by diversity of soil, tree-growth and other conditions affecting the production and development of forest-trees.

(2) Then the best plan of laying out roads and avenues, which will have to be constructed for the transportation of timber and other wood products, has to be deliberately considered. This is one of the most important works for the future management of the woods. It should be entrusted only to a person who is theoretically and practically fully conversant with such operations. For it is not sufficient to lay out one or more roads to satisfy the transient and local wants which have chanced to spring up; but the entire interests of the forest in its present and future condition as well as those of its environs have to be looked after, and a road system has to be devised which, although not yet fully required, will be necessary in the future when the woods are more developed, and the time arrives that the wood products will be utilized to their fullest extent.

(3) A wooded region to be taken in hand, and to be worked systematically, should after the completion of the operations indicated in 1 and 2, be laid out in districts containing from 100,000 to 150,000 acres, and subdivided in smaller ones of from 10 to 20,000 acres. While the whole tract would be supervised by one Over-forester, the subdivisions should be under the continual care and attention of

a forester, acquainted with the methods of the routine work, who should, according to the directions given by the Over-forester, superintend the working force of laborers employed in cutting and removing the wood products, or in cultivating and planting denuded stretches within the district. The Forest Officials should have a permanent residence within their territory, and it should be their duty to guard the place against fire and trespass, for which purpose they should have the power to arrest trespassers.

The boundaries of the districts, and their subdivisions, may be formed either naturally by old roads, streams, ditches, adjoining open fields, etc., or artificially by opening avenues and roads. Under all circumstances, adjoining forests belonging to different owners should be separated by a clearing of trees along the boundaries, about one rod wide, to which each party should contribute one-half of the space so that a properly indicated boundary line would run in the midst of this path.

(4) After the above-mentioned labors have been completed the first and most effective step to be taken in order to transform a wild wood into a cultivated forest, is to thin it out, that is, to cut and remove all inferior vegetation and dead trees as well as those that encroach upon the quick development of the more desirable trees; but with the restriction that the soil may not be exposed to sunlight and atmospheric influences.* In order to enable the laborers to do this work efficiently, the subdivisions of the forests should be cut up in *blocks* containing from 3 to 400 acres, and separated by a clearing or path about eighteen or twenty feet wide, called in German "Schneissen," upon which the output of the block can be removed.

(5) When the roads and avenues in a large forest have been established and made practicable, we can go on cut-

---

* See page 111. sqq

ting and removing all mature and overmature trees, observing as far as possible the restriction made by thinning out the woods, viz., to preserve the natural soil conditions to the best of our ability.

(6) While in cutting and removing wood products out of the forests the rule of performing this work with the greatest care and regard toward the adjoining tree-growth has to be strictly obeyed (see p. 114. i.f.); the felling itself should be done so as to promote a natural reproduction according to the directions given in Chapter XII. But where this is impracticable—and this will often happen in wild woods—there should be no delay in establishing forest nurseries, not only for rearing the required seedlings for restocking or filling out denuded wood areas; but also for collecting at the proper times ripe seeds from the most desirable kinds of trees in the whole forest. A good gardener, well versed in the culture of trees, will prove fully competent to manage such a concern.

Thus it will be seen that the possible absence of men fully acquainted with the methods of scientific forestry should not prevent us from the introduction of a rational treatment of our wild woods, as every thing that has to be done during the first four or five years before scientific methods may be employed, can be perfectly done by our own citizens without any prejudice to the future management. In the mean time, if it should be necessary to employ skilled foresters, enough of them will probably be found.*

---

* The report of the State Forest Commission for 1886, on page 17. i.f., contends that scientifically educated foresters cannot be obtained here. This statement is not supported by facts, as skilled foresters are very often, through the advertising columns of the New York newspapers, seeking employment. Certainly they do not find it in the management of woods, because such a thing like that does not exist here; but they embark in allied employments, especially in agriculture. However, as soon as the State will introduce a systematic management

By inducing our State to enlarge its wooded area in the Adirondacks and to introduce there a methodical management, we should urge this measure for the sole reason, that this is the only means to preserve the forest-growth upon the woodlands containing the watersheds of our principal rivers *permanently*, and that without a permanent forest-growth upon these lands, the continuance of a regular water-flow to the rivers would be greatly endangered. That the State woods will yield lateron a revenue, if managed on business principles, cannot be doubted. But we should not expect such a result during the next generation. The income obtained at present by European Governments from their well-managed forests, may serve as an example of what a well-conducted administration of forests may be able to perform. However, it would be a very erroneous conception of the present desolate condition of our State forests and of the wide disproportion between the value of lumber and the cost of both labor and transportation, as we find in our country, if we should expect with the introduction of a methodical forest management, to at once obtain the same pecuniary results which the European governments have realized through a well-organized forest

---

of its forests, there will be made undoubtedly many offers to serve the commonwealth.

In this connection it may be of interest to our forestry students to learn that the tendency of European experts in sylviculture, contrary to former practices in the management of forests, is lately directed to a more close observation of Nature's workings in the wild forests. They try now to sustain their theories from facts suggested to them by Nature, rather than to follow the narrow paths outlined by old authorities. Whereas formerly the European forester advocated the cultivation of forests with pure stock, divided in blocks with adequate revolutions of cutting and replanting, the present generation acknowledges in many respects the great advantages of the natural woods, and recommends now in the establishment of new forests, *mixed planting*, and in their exploitation the *selection of single trees*, instead of the former complete clearing of entire wood areas.

service with the greatest exertions during the last fifty years.

What we may reasonably expect, is to bring our woods after continued and well-directed operations during the first decade, to a condition in which they may prove self-supporting. Having reached this point, with which a great benefit to our State will be gained—see pages 25 and 26—we may be confident, that enlarged knowledge and experience of our Forest Officials in matters of scientific Forestry will render our State forests from year to year more profitable, with a steadily improving condition of the forests; so that the next century may witness such an increase of the wealth to our State from this single source, as we are now entirely unable to imagine. People will then bless those men who undauntedly persisted in establishing a State industry, by which not only the commonwealth derived a handsome income, but which also created the opening of a new and honorable career to many men for profitable employment. This condition of things will be the more gratifying as the people will not be taxed for the support of a small army of Forest Officials and laborers; they will be paid by the profits derived from their operations in the culture of the forest, and they will earn much more than they expend.

In conclusion, a few remarks in regard to the nomenclature used in the science of forestry might be well-timed.

Forestry, as applied on the European Continent, being an entirely unknown science in England and its dependencies, it is not to be wondered at that the English language has no designations appropriate to the technical words and methods of managing forests recognized in European forest economy. We, therefore, in introducing systematic forestry in our country, have mostly to fall back upon the expressions applied in Europe, till we have advanced so far as to establish our own system of designation. In the mean time we should apply those words, which although now used indiscriminately in forestry matters, are able to recive a specific technical signification in a confined and appropriate meaning. First among them is the word "forest." It is in English used as being identical with "woods;" and yet it would be a great linguistic improvement, if we would only apply it to those woods, which are cultivated and systematically managed; and leave the expression "woods" to the wild or naturally grown-up woods. We would then very properly speak of the North *woods* of the Adirondacks, but very improperly, when designating them as wild or natural "*forests*."

PART II.—Forest Planting on Plains.

Having treated in the foregoing part of general matters of forest culture, we will now consider the various kinds of forest planting.

All forest vegetation is dependent, not only upon the climate of the country, but also upon the soil and location The State of New York is especially favored in its situation, as its climate is moderated by the close proximity to the Atlantic Ocean, a circumstance that increases the humidity of the generally very dry air, and causes a snow, and rainfall sufficient to produce a luxurious forest-growth. Woods, therefore, have sprung up all over the State, except in those places where the soil is too poor to bring forth any vegetation at all, and the variety of trees of spontaneous growth is larger here than in any other State of the Union by reason of the many varieties of soil and diversities of elevation, the latter in many cases reaching heights where only bushes and shrubs grow.

As the vegetation on the plains shows a marked difference from that on the mountains, both in regard to varieties and treatment, we have to consider them separately and wili take up first, Forest Planting on Plains.

CHAPTER I.

FOREST PLANTING ON LANDS WITH ALLUVIAL SOIL.

IN our State we have a great amount of alluvial soil formed by the deposits of the many rivers and rivulets which descend from our hills and mountains. This soil mostly contains such favorable mixture of earthy and mineral substances as to promote all vegetation to the highest degree—and on such places, agriculture lays its exclusive and well-founded claims. But there are among them many low sites which, being subjected to oft-repeated inundations, cannot be used for agricultural purposes, and yet may be utilized advantageously for the cultivation of willows.

Although the willow is not considered as being a forest-tree proper, the management of large forests, especially that of mountain forests, requires often the propagation and cultivation of willows on an extensive scale, because they chiefly furnish the material to bind the drifting sand, and to hold the loose soil along the banks of streams in place. For this purpose—as we will see in Part III—those kinds are cultivated which retain their shape as shrubs; while the tree-like kinds are used to serve as pollards, (see page 132 Note*). The propagation is effected by cuttings—see page 67—and in the management of the willow shrubs along the banks of rivers, exposed to inundations we resort to a coppice treatment with short rotations from eight to ten years, the rods retaining up to that age the pliability, by which they are able to withstand the pressure of the invading waters, and to break their force without being broken themselves. If they are allowed to grow older, they lose their flexibility, and becoming stiff and immovable, the intruding waters create behind them whirlpools which undermine the soft soil, and form pools with stagnant water, by which not only the further plant-growth but also the consistency of the bank is endangered. What kinds of willows of the many indigenous species we should employ for the purposes stated, will be best learned from experience made in the different localities of our State in regard to the growth and behavior of the same. That our indigenous species are not of great economic value especially for osier purposes is pretty certain, as their twigs and rods are mostly wanting the flexibility which renders them so useful in basket-making. To furnish the required material for this growing industry we therefore have had for years to look—and are still looking upon importations of rods from Germany. Lately, however, the cultivation of some of the foreign species having met with success here, we are now able to advantageously employ a culture by which many areas of lands may be made profitable which otherwise would be entirely useless.

The willows mostly used in Germany for industrial purposes are: *salix purpurea* and *viminalis*. The latter grows tree-like, while the former develops into shrubs. *Salix viminalis* produces a much larger quantity of twigs, and strong ones at that, which farmers use for building fences. *Salix purpurea* is by far not so coarse as *viminalis* and, therefore especially in demand for the manufacture of the finer grades of willow-ware. In our State the *salix purpurea* is called the red osier, and although imported from Germany, succeeds very well. It produces numerous pliant, evenly grown rods which are especially adapted for wattling purposes. This willow, the bark of which furnishes also the material for extracting salicylic acid, is not so fastidious in regard to the soil, growing well not only on moist but also on dry, sandy soil, and even on swampy lands. It can endure the heat and cold as well as moisture and dryness. The profits of a willow plantation are very large. In Germany they used to be as high as $80 per acre. The cultivation is comparatively easy. The natural homes of the willow are the banks of rivers and the low bottom lands subjected to temporary inundations. The soil best adapted for a permanent willow plantation is a moist humus with a sandy subsoil. There is no kind of tree with which water plays so important a part as the willow. It is true the willow likes a moist soil which may sometimes be even entirely overflowed, but the water should not remain for too long a time and, therefore, in places where this occurs, drainage should be resorted to.

Willow plantations require a thorough cultivation with deep plowing and subsoiling to the depth of 18 inches. If expenses are no obstacle, spading in such a way as to turn the subsoil up and spread it over the humus is to be preferred. Then the roots of the young plants have the benefit of the fertile soil, while the infertile subsoil on the top prevents the growth of weeds. For spring planting—and this is in our State preferable to fall planting—the ground should be fully prepared during the preceding fall before the first frost appears and exposed to the action of the frost and air during the winter. The cuttings should be made late in the fall, when vegetation has come to rest, about 12 inches long, from vigorous and sound main shoots, using only the lower half of them. They should be kept during the winter, bundled up in moist sand in a place which is free from frost. They are planted from one to two feet apart in rows, which are wide enough to allow the soil between them to be worked, in order to eradicate the weeds. The best way to keep the plantation clean, and at the same time to secure a rapid growth, is to manure the space between the rows and raise therein potatoes, turnips, or other root-fruits which require a good deal of cultivation during the summer. If this system be practiced, there will be already in the second year shoots so large as to allow a crop. Large plantations, however, are commonly divided into three to four fields (lots), of which one is cut every year. This short rotation is preferred, because the rods when young are more pliable than when growing older. In planting the cuttings, care should be taken, not to disturb the callus, which had been formed at the bottom of the cuttings during the time of their being bundled up and covered with moist sand. They should be set at an angle of forty-five degrees in the plant hole with the eyes in an upward direction. Cuttings planted in this way are much better packed in the ground by the settling of the soil than when set straight up, and there is nothing which hurts the growth of cuttings more than becoming loose in the soil and being shaken by the wind. See page 67.

CHAPTER II.

FOREST PLANTING ON MARSHY OR SWAMPY LANDS.

THERE are many acres of bottom land along the rivers, which, owing to their low situation, cannot be drained. Upon them there soon appear sour grasses, reeds, rushes and sedges, out of the decaying materials of which and of other vegetable and mineral accretions the bogs, marshes or fens and swamps are formed.

Wet grounds are called either bogs or marshes or swamps. *Bogs* are the softest grounds, and often too soft to bear a man. *Marshes* or *fens* are less soft, but very wet; however, they bear a man. *Swamps* are soft and spongy but sustain man and beast, and are often pastured. The subsoil, mostly, is of sandy structure. If these wet grounds contain a good proportion of minerals and mineral combinations with vegetable matter, they afford the best opportunity for raising every cultivated fruit. But commonly this kind of soil is too porous and does not possess the consistency required by plant vegetation for its vigorous growth. Should it be possible to overcome this obstacle by adding sand or clay to the surface soil there is no artificial meadow which will, under proper treatment, produce more grass and fodder than such a natural meadow. If such meadows can be drained even only by forming raised beds, with deep ditches, every crop could be successfully raised upon them. But most localities of this kind cannot be drained, and being exposed to repeated inundations by rivers, there is no other means of utilizing them than by growing forest-trees. The preparation of the soil, in this case consists in burning over the top of the soil, in doing which, care has to be taken that the fire should not penetrate too deeply into the soil and consume the entire vegetable mould, for then the soil would lose most of its fertility, and produce only shrubs and mullen stalks. But if only the top of the surface soil is burnt, the mixing of the ashes with the remaining soil renders it very fertile, and planting may be begun in the following spring.

Another means to prepare swampy grounds for tree culture is to dig out narrow but deep ditches at the proper distance apart, and spread the dugout upon the beds thus formed. The softer the field, the deeper the trenches should be dug, and consequently the higher should the beds be raised. Although there is much left for one's own judgment in this matter, the proportion of the width of beds to that of the ditches usually is five to one, while the depth of the ditches is regulated by the depth of the vegetable mould and the level of the ground-water. The ditches should be so deep as to bring up a layer of the sandy subsoil at least six inches thick, and heighten the beds to such a degree that the level of the ground-water remains at least three feet below the surface soil. After the lapse of one year, planting may be begun without any further working of the soil, the heavy sand sinking by its own weight into the porous surface, thus rendering it fit for sylvi-culture. But should the dugup subsoil be loamy, a thorough plowing and mixing with the top soil is necessary. On the soil of a swamp prepared in this manner, "*planting*" of forest-trees is decidedly preferable to "*seeding*" as such ground invites the growth of grasses too much, and, therefore, the surface will soon be covered by a dense mat of grass and weeds unless more often disturbed by the cultivator, a treatment which would in a seeded field prevent the seeds from sprouting. The best time for planting is the spring, as by planting during the fall, winter killing could not be avoided on account of the elevated lay of the spongy beds, and their being greatly exposed to frost. But even to plant seedlings (from one to two years old) the rapidity of the growth of grass and weeds is very obnoxious, and, therefore, to prevent any inroads from this cause, hill-planting has to be resorted to.* In these hills, made from the subsoil earth, the seedlings are set as

---

*See pages 97 and 98.

deep as possible without covering the top of the hill. Upon swamps containing rich soil should be planted spruces, oaks and beeches, with which ash, elm and maple, may be mixed. On such places the most lucrative forest management for producing timber and lumber can be introduced, as here also all valuable light-needing trees prosper and grow so strongly that even an intermixture of the otherwise much dreaded birch may be permitted.

If the soil of the swamp is poor, spruces and oaks may be planted under the protection of the pine. On sloughs, that is, swamps with such wet ground as cannot be drained at all, the swamp hickory, alder and black ash will still thrive, and even the spruce and balsam fir will grow and exercise a beneficient effect in absorbing the moisture of the ground and rendering it more compact.

CHAPTER III.

FOREST PLANTING ON MOORLANDS.

Leaving the low bottom lands of the rivers—called the alluvium—and ascending to the higher plains we find, that, in the original state of the country, a few kinds of the Erica family take possession of the territory both dry and wet, and form the principal vegetation. Only where the ground is too sandy and loose do they give way to lichens, mosses and other plants which are content with very poor soil, as for instance, small leaved winter dock, corn marigold etc. Those Ericas possess the peculiarity of secreting through their leaves much resin, and this combined with the rotten roots and other parts of the plants, bring into existence in the course of time, so thick and impenetrable a surface soil that neither rain nor any other moisture of the air or earth can sink into the ground. Moreover, should any elevation of the ground prevent the stagnant waters from flowing off, swamps are formed which foster the growth of aquatic plants (cotton-grasses, tuft-grasses, etc.), by the decay and rotting of which the organic surface of the soil is continually increased. This is the way in which the so-called moorlands are built up. When the accumulations of aquatic plants have reached a considerable height the power of vegetation passes away and peat bogs of more or less consistency are formed according to whether the water is drained off or retained in the soil. In the lowlands of the heaths this soil is often mixed with more or less muck.* Should it be possible to apply drainage here, there would be an opportunity for cultivating every kind of grain. But if moorlands do not contain anything to counteract the noxious effect of the too abundant carbonaceous humus and humic acid, there is no other means of utilizing such lands except to prepare them for raising forest-trees, and, for this purpose, to mix with the moor soil the deeper lying mineralic ingredients of the subsoil. This is done in the following manner: After the moor has been drained as much as practicable the tufts of the top soil are scattered all over, and the surface is, as much as possible, made level. Thereupon deep plowing is resorted to with the effect of bringing up the sand from the subsoil for mixing it with the moor dirt. Should the moor layer be so thick that

*We mean by "muck" the vegetable deposits of swamps and ponds, consisting of decayed organic substances mixed with more or less earth and containing much carbon.

the subsoil cannot be reached by the plow, then sand should be dug up from the bottom of the ditches, running through the moor, and scattered over the surface soil, whereupon by deep plowing a complete mixing of the surface soil with the dugout sand should be perfected. If the surface soil be pretty compact and strong, a sand layer from five to six inches thick will be sufficient, while poorer soil should be enriched by a layer several inches thicker.

This culture *may be* preceded by burning over the surface soil, by which process the expenses of the cultivation are remarkably lessened. But if the turf (top of the moor soil) proves to be very thick, burning over the surface soil cannot be avoided, but *must* be, under all circumstances, employed.

When the surface of a moor has been treated in this way, the spruce, and even fir, may be planted as principal stock of trees; as the soil, even during the driest summers, will contain sufficient moisture to favor the growth of these trees. According to the quality of the soil, either beeches and oaks, or oaks and pines, or only pines are used to serve as mixture, the best soil been assigned to the first-named trees and the next best to the second combination. The poorest soil will not permit the growth of any other kind of trees but the pine. However, under the cover of this tree there may spruce and hemlock grow, although they will not flourish luxuriantly.

CHAPTER IV.

FOREST PLANTING ON HIGH MOORS.

It is an undisputed fact that an area covered with the richest humus, if exposed to continual moisture, will soon lose its fertility, and all plant-life on it will die, as the stagnant water thoroughly chills the soil and leeches out every particle of plant-food. Upon the remains of the destroyed vegetation, first peat-mosses, and later, more developed aquatic plants make their appearance. These continually die off, only to let others spring up again, and in the fulness of time, they reach such an elevated position as to be in want of necessary humidity. The remainder of these plants, on account of their submersion and of the antiseptic property of the humic acid contained in the water do not fully decay, but accumulate during many years and finally form a thick moss-turf (cover of the moor) upon which some of the ericaeas appear, together with other plants which are content with a moist moor ground and sour humus. As long as the bottom of a moor is being raised by this accretion, the moor extends further on over the margins and becomes larger, for the original vegetation of the borders also dies out, owing to the increased swampy condition into which the surrounding margin of the moor has been brought, giving way to the mosses. The central part of these moors, having grown up for a longer time than the margins (which always extend laterally) usually has a higher situation than the borders and is, therefore, called in Germany High Moor and in England Moss-land. The vegetation thereon principally consists of peat-mosses and heath-plants, of which the former occupy the low, swampy places, while the latter settle upon the comparatively higher and, therefore, drier and more compact parts of the moor—the tufts

The first annual report of the New York Forest Commission contains the following graphic description of these moors which are called there "natural meadows." "These natural meadows are formed by the gradual filling-up of lake or pond-beds with an accumulated growth and deposit. They are seen in the Adirondacks in all stages of formation; some having a wide swampy margin with a matted growth of aquatic vegetation; and others still, entirely grown over. The last stage of development is the natural meadow, level as a floor, on which grows a scant, wiry, inferior quality of grass."

The high moors or moss lands are formed not only on plains and on heaths, but also in forests and upon mountains, covered with a luxuriant growth of forest-trees. This is proved by the many large trees which are found in the peat layers. In former years the beavers, by building their dams across the forest streams, laid the foundation for many high moors. At present, reckless men, who undertake to transport felled trees by rafts upon the torrents of mountains, often stop the natural flow of the waters, by erecting dams, and cause a back flow which kills even the most luxurious forest-growth, forming a nucleus around which the rapacious aquatic plants gather and work up their way in the above described manner. On this subject the cited Report of the New York Forest Commission also contains a vivid description which we think will be very interesting to the reader. Under the heading of *Beaver Meadows* it says, on page 19, "Years ago when the beavers were plenty in the Adirondack waters, they built their dams across the creeks and streams. Sometimes these dams caused long back flows, covering the low ground where the stream was sluggish and the fall slight. The surrounding trees and bushes, water-killed or drowned by the back flow, or gnawed down by the beavers, fell into the water and gradually decayed. This mixed with the débris brought by floods, as time went on, filled their pond, and aquatic vegetation, finding root in this rich mould, soon completed the work."

In regard to the cultivation of the high moors the following considerations may be kept in view: The peat-mosses form an infertile soil and wherever the top soil consists of such ingredients there is no possibility for a successful culture of forest vegetation. But the heath plants render the moor soil compact, and even enrich it, forming in due time a surface soil which proves the more nutritous the thicker it becomes, and enables us to proceed with growing forest-trees thereon. In Europe those countries which contain many high-moors are very poor and, therefore, only sparsely settled. But lately the moors have been recommended for planting them with forest-trees and people have successfully grown there all kinds of trees, especially oak seedlings as coppice wood for tanning purposes.

For raising forest-trees upon high moors, first of all there has to be ascertained whether mineralic earth may be had from the subsoil without too much expense. If this be the case, the culture upon raised beds as described in Chapter II. would be the most advisable one. The more mosses the top soil contains and consequently the poorer this soil is, the more sand has to be brought up from the subsoil and thoroughly mixed with the moor soil. Commonly a layer of sand from 6 to 10 inches will be sufficient. Should the moor ground be too deep to reach the sandy subsoil, drainage combined with burning over the top soil is the only means for unlocking the plant-producing power of the ground. High moors which have been burnt over are very favorably changed, both in regard to the mechanical and chemical conditions of the soil. Naturally the peaty ground is too porous to retain moisture and, therefore, in dry weather parches up while it, by a continuance of rain, is converted into a mud pool. After the surplus water has been drained off and the top soil burnt over, the ground becomes more compact and, for this reason, does not change so much by alternate drying up and being overflowed with water. In this condition of greater density the soil is still enabled to let in the gases of the air, required for the support of every vegetation, and to easily absorb moisture from the atmosphere to supply the demands of the plants. Such soil does not retain so much water as thereby to kill the plant-roots in case of frost. The chemical condition of this soil is, by the burning in so far improved, as many of the elements obnoxious to plant-growth, are destroyed while others enter into combinations which are favoring plant-growth. So the too abundant humic acid disappears and leaves a carbonate of lime which serves to further take out the sourness of the ground. The protoxide or black oxide, which is always found in great quantities on such places and poisons every plant, takes up, after the water is removed, more oxygen, and is then changed into the unnoxious peroxide, or red iron which even furnishes some food to plants.

As for the trees to be planted after the high moors have received the proper preparation, it has been proved to be best, to plant upon sanded moor ground principally the spruce, to which may be added oak and pine. Upon the not sanded moors, pine is the leading tree, to which the spruce and, in a small scale, the oak may be added as mixtures.

Drainage and burning over the surface soil being the principal means to bring the moors into such a condition as to plant forest-trees upon them, are, therefore, so important that they may well form the subject of a special consideration.

CHAPTER V.

DRAINAGE.

WHEN moors are to be prepared for tree-growth, the first step to accomplish this end is to apply drainage. By this it is not intended to remove all of the humidity out of the ground, but only the *excess* of water—a water-soaked soil being detrimental to every plant-growth.

In bottom-lands, drainage is often dammed up by the high water-table of adjoining rivers, but the hilly uplands afford ample opportunity for the application of this improvement.

In order to render the drainage of a place or district perfect, a careful investigation of the entire locality should be instituted, and its topography, including the courses of the streams and rivers, should be minutely mapped out. Thereupon the elevations of the surface and the height of the water-table should be found out and marked on the map or chart.

After the level of the place, both in regard to its principal part and the adjuncts, has been ascertained, a system of drains and their operation, by which the excess of water may be let off, can be easily delineated. First, an appropriate direction has to be given to the main or receiving ditch. Commonly, this direction will point to the more inclined part of the place, and the outlet will be the spot which is situated lowest.

On most of extended tracts, we find empty beds of old rivulets or other water courses. These are the best guides for ascertaining the natural level of the place. However, the site and run of the river, stream or other channel, into which the principal ditch is supposed to pass off its contents, is the decisive moment in settling the question of the direction of this ditch. If feasible, the direction should be the *straightest possible,* not only for the sake of saving territory and labor, but because the flow of water is then less damaging to the slopes of the ditch than when checked by curvatures and windings.

In order to determine upon the width and depth of the main ditch, the quantity of water which runs over the place not only during summer time, but also during floods and in wet seasons must be ascertained. Finally, an examination of the quality of the soil, especially in regard to its different layers, ingredients, water-table, porosity, etc., must be made, because the correct laying out of the trenches depends for the most part upon these considerations.

In planning out the particulars of a drainage system for moors there should not only be taken into consideration the best way to let off the water, and to prevent forever the degeneration of moors into swamps, but also the means to stop the outflow during the dry seasons at will. If the subsoil be sandy, a deepening of the level of the ground water sometimes becomes highly objectionable because the vegetation in such case, during a dry season, will not be so sufficiently developed as it would be if the necessary humidity of the soil were retained.

Usually forest-trees thrive where the land extends

from three to four feet above the level of the ground water, although a great many trees send their roots much deeper into the soil. But if the moor is very spongy and porous, there exists such a capillary attraction of the ground water up to the overlaying soil, that with the lowering of the water-table to the stated depth, the necessary drainage and percolation of air through the soil cannot be obtained. It is, therefore, advisable to lay the main ditch, if possible, deep enough so as to bring the water-table to a level with the *solid* subsoil. The danger that the surface soil, by this arrangement, may be rendered too dry will be avoided, as hereinbefore stated, by the erection of proper devices for stopping the flow of water at will.

The main ditch should be laid out in the deepest places of the longitudinal fall of the area, and into this ditch the side-ditches open so as to discharge their water at the most acute angle possible. The side ditches are mostly laid out pretty regular, except if springs or other aqueous spots should be found for the drainage of which special trenches should be opened. If the area to be drained extends more in breadth than in length, especially if the middle part contains an elevation running straight through the middle and is sloping on both sides of the centrum of the area, no side ditches are required, but only several longitudinal ditches, running parallel or nearly so with the main ditch, may be opened, provided they are situated so near to each other as to drain off, completely, the water of the land lying between them.

The number of side ditches depends upon the quantity of the water to be drained off and the condition of the soil, while the depth of the ditches depends upon the elevation of the soil and the quantity of water to be carried by the ditch. Owing to the pressure exercised by the surrounding soil upon the sides of the ditches, danger exists of the embankments sliding down and, ere long, to fill up the ditches. For this reason the sides of the ditches have to slope at an angle of about 35° from the horizontal, whether the soil may consist of sand, clay or loam. For, although the soil of the last-named kind stands for a while firm, if the sides of a ditch are all perpendicular, the drying effect of the air upon the sides is such as to soon remove every tenacity out of the soil, and make it crumble down into the ditch.

The slope of ditches in moors with tenacious soil used to be from 15° to 30° from the perpendicular; with loose soil 45° ; and if there is reason to assume that the quantity of water carried through will be very large and rapid, a slope of 60° to 70° is to be given. The base of the ditches is commonly as wide as the ditch is deep, unless the locality, especially the elevation of the soil, renders a change necessary. From the depth, the width of the base and the pitch of the sides it is easy to compute the amount of area occupied by the ditch. It is of great importance to establish a uniform grade of descent in the slope of the ditches. The larger the bulk of the water is which has to pass off, the greater the force of the water in the duct (or conduit) becomes, and the less the gradual fall should be, especially in loose soils ; otherwise the bottom and slopes of the ditches will be exposed to the danger of washing out. In case the natural descent should be too steep and, therefore, encroachments upon the slopes are apprehended, it is necessary to interrupt the descent from time to time, and to establish little rapids in the ditches at the foot of which a new grade commences. But this operation seldom occurs in the plains; it is applied mostly in hilly regions.

In large, extended plains a fall of 1.6000 may be sufficient for a regular flow of the water; usually the proportion of 1.2000 is considered desirable for the proper discharge of the water, and in smaller ditches even a greater fall may be given without danger of injury to the base or sides of the ditches.

The transverse ditches which discharge their water into the main ditch should have the least possible fall, because, if thus constructed, they can easily be shut up whenever required and the water therein retained during a dry season. Usually they are so planned that during the wet seasons they discharge the water at a proper depth, while during the dry summer seasons, the water in the main ditch is stopped and forced to flow back into the lateral ditches, in order to furnish the soil with the necessary moisture. This is especially desirable in sandy soils.

The above suggestions may be sufficient for guidance in draining smaller areas, and where no great local difficulties have to be overcome. However, where the project assumes larger dimensions, and the obstacles to be surmounted are of more than usual magnitude, an expert should be called in for surveying, mapping and laying out the field, while the employer will be greatly assisted by the rules hereinbefore given to ascertain that the planning and execution of the work will prove satisfactory.

CHAPTER VI.

BURNING OVER THE SOIL FOR CULTIVATION.

THERE does not exist any mode of cultivating the soil which the agriculturist despises more than that which is done by burning over the surface ground. And yet there is no means by which the natural or wild moors may be brought into the proper condition for growing upon them forest-trees more cheaply and quickly than just this primitive operation. We, therefore, may be permitted to treat upon this subject a little more extensively.

After the moor has been sufficiently drained, beds about fifty feet wide are laid out and enclosed with ditches twelve inches deep. In the fall or early winter, preceding the burning, the rugged surface soil is broken up with a *hand* hoe, the iron of which should be tapering and curved on the inside. By this action the peaty tufts become inverted and the top soil assumes a pretty even form. During the ensuing winter the frost acts upon the clods making them more friable. In the next spring the work of hoeing over the surface is repeated for the effect of pulverizing the clods thoroughly, and of making the top on the lower parts of the moor as even as possible, whereby the laborers are instructed to work the soil so as to make a little ridge in the middle of the beds in order that the atmospheric moistures may flow off more quickly. Thereupon the moor is allowed to rest several weeks till the surface has become thoroughly dry. After this the ground is often worked with a *hand* harrow—for working with farm animals would be impossible upon such a light and spongy soil—till the top becomes fully dried to the depth of about eight inches. On a warm, sunny day in early summer burning over the peaty ground begins, and for that purpose little heaps of the lightest and dryest soil, in distances of from forty to fifty feet, are raked up and kindled in such a way that the heaps lying to the windward are ignited first. When these heaps are fairly burning, panfuls of the burning soil are taken up and the ignited turf is scattered all over the spaces between the heaps till the whole area is on fire. The operation is generally done during the noontime, when wind and heat are strong, and in such manner that the operator commences kindling from that part of the moor which is situated in the face of the wind, working up his way against the wind. In doing so the fire penetrates from three to four inches into the soil and leaves an ash layer of the same thickness. As soon as the fire has done its work and the smoke is cleared away, the best we can do to make the moor pay for the expenses caused by this culture, is to sow buckwheat even upon the warm ashes, as this grain, under favorable circumstances, may yield the richest crop ever harvested. The best time of sowing is at the end of May. The sowing is done by hand, whereupon with a light hand harrow, the grain is covered and rolled over by a *hand* roller. Early in fall, when most of the buckwheat kernels have turned black, the crop is cut and left in the field in swaths until dry enough to be put into little heaps, which, when perfectly dry, are placed in the barn.

Every spring during the next three years, the ditches should be deepened in the same proportion as the surface soil is lowered by the burning, in order to keep the ditches at a uniform depth of about twelve inches; and the moor should be worked with a common, perforated *hand* hoe and burnt over again. Buckwheat will still be the most profitable crop, paying nearly all the expenses that have been incurred for the improvement. The moor will then be in such a condition as to produce for several years a crop of oats or rye; but it is best not to exhaust the fertility of the soil too much, and rather let it rest and enter upon a fallow of several years, after which forest-planting may be commenced successfully. At all events, the soil, by the several burnings and cultivatings, will be chemically so much changed that its obnoxious ingredients are destroyed, and components favorable for plant-growth which formerly were locked up, become unlocked and efficient. Precautions have, however, to be taken not to burn too deep into the moor-ground, because only the heath plantation should be destroyed, while the underlying inactive elements which originated from the decayed aquatic plants will be brought into use by the drainage. For this reason the fires should run over the top soil as quickly as possible, and, therefore, the ignition be made when the weather is very dry and fresh winds are blowing. It is true that then the ashes are lost, but the residue of the coals is what stimulates the vitality of the underlying soil. In order to prevent damages which may occur when the fire penetrates too deep into the earth it is advisable to close the ditches so as to keep the water-table up to a desired height.

CHAPTER VII.

FOREST PLANTING ON SAND-WASTES OR PINE-BARRENS.

In our State we have many varieties of sandy soils, which contain principally silicates, without a proper admixture of the other minerals (clay, lime, potash) necessary for a thrifty vegetable growth. Moreover the mechanical texture of such grounds is entirely unqualified to retain humidity, as this either disappears by evaporation or by sinking into the depths of the soil, where it is inaccessible to the roots of plants. The only way to utilize such lands is to grow forest-trees upon them, as experience shows us that upon soils containing nearly ninety-eight per cent. pure sand and almost no water * pines and oaks may be successfully grown, unless climate and situation prevent the growth of any plant-vegetation.

In the European territories most of the sand-wastes, excepting blowing sands, are covered with a mat of heaths, whins and brooms, through which water penetrates but sparsely into the ground. This mat which is from three to five inches deep, usually rests upon an impenetrable stratum, from eight to twelve inches thick, which consists of sand cemented by calcareous and vegetable matter or by iron oxide. This hard-pan or heath-pan, in Germany called "Orstein," which is formed by acidification of the subsoil, and is underlaid with sand, must first be broken, and the broken pieces must be brought to the surface in order that the air may desoxide them and remove the elements obnoxious to plant-growth contained therein. After this has been effected, plant-

* The far-famed forest of Fontainebleau, in France, is grown on just such kind of soil.

ing can be begun. But as this kind of soil is not often met with in our State, we will leave it out of further consideration, and turn to the common sand-wastes, of which there are, as the census of 1880 says, several millions of acres.

In order to bring the sand-wastes proper (excepting the blowing or shifting or drifting sands) in a condition adapted for raising trees upon them, the soil should receive one deep plowing in the fall preceding the planting, and, after being harrowed, should be left untouched during the ensuing winter. Early in spring, planting or seeding—as the cultivator may have decided upon—can be commenced.

Regarding the selection of the trees to be planted, there is no doubt that the pine will be the dominant species. But as in sandy soils constant protection of the ground against the drying influences of sun and wind has to be principally aimed at; and as the pine, after a growth of from ten to fifteen years, loses its side branches, with which it effects this protection, spruce, oak and even beeches should be mixed in the proportion of one-fifth of spruces, and of one-tenth of oaks and beeches. In case seedlings are set out, it is easy to determine upon the proper place for each tree. But when the ground is to be seeded—and, over large areas, sowing is by far cheaper and more quickly accomplished, although it is not so sure during the first growing period of the seedlings—furrows have to be opened, in which the nuts of oaks and beeches are sown, whereupon the field should be harrowed even. Then the pine and spruce seed is sown broadcast and lightly harrowed under. On very light soil this operation has the effect of causing the several kinds of trees to spring up easily and to continue growing until first the beech, then the oak, and finally the spruce disappears for want of plant-food; while the pine remains as the stock of standard trees. On the better sandy soils, containing a larger amount of clay, lime, etc., the pine is destined to preserve the humidity of the soil, and to protect its co-plants against sun and wind. In this case, therefore, the management should be so directed as to eliminate the evergreens as soon as the deciduous trees have reached the proper age and condition that will enable them to shift for themselves in light soil, and at the same time to constantly protect the soil against sun and wind. For such kind of ground preserves its increasing fertility only when *continually* protected against atmospheric influences, whereas a removal of the trees and the exposure of the soil to the effects of sun and air make the recovered fertility of the ground disappear very soon. Conclusive evidence of the truth of this assertion is furnished by the present condition of the "Landes of Sologne," in France, a barren sand-waste of 100,000 acres, only interrupted by marshes and swamps. And yet history tells us that these "Landes" formerly were covered with a dense forest. Avarice and imprudence of men cleared the woods away, and the "Landes" relapsed into what was their original condition. Therefore, care must be taken to at once replant vacancies and glades with oaks, beeches, hornbeams, etc., at small distances apart—from four to six feet; and to renew stunted or damaged single trees by strong seedlings. Openings in plantations of very light soil should be filled out with spruces.

It is, therefore, justly contended that sand-wastes can be reclaimed by sylviculture, because they obtain thereby a fertility which afterwards enables them to produce grain for some time. As soon as this fertility has given out, we have it in our power to regain the lost fertility by reforesting the sand-wastes.

CHAPTER VIII.

FOREST PLANTING ON INLAND SAND-DRIFTS.

THE difficulties which have to be overcome in order to aforest sand-wastes or pine-barrens, are, as we have seen in the preceding chapter, not inconsiderable. And yet they will be still greater and nearly insurmountable when sand-drifts or blowing sands are to be brought into a condition which shall render them suitable for sylviculture. In general there are two different phases in which sand-drifts are met with. One form is that of *barren plains* in the interior of our State, another that of the *downs or dunes*, that is: the shifting hillocks upon the sea coast. Undoubtedly the former have been in times long past fixed naturally by arboreous growth; while the sand-drifts on the sea coast never have been covered with any substantial vegetation.

The inland sand-drifts can be brought into cultivation after the mobile sand on the surface of the barren plains has been bound or fixed. This operation is accomplished by, first, making the ground as even as possible, and then laying over it in a chessboard-like way, sods taken from old pastures or peatbogs, whereupon the whole tract—both the covered and the uncovered part of it—is seeded down with grasses which check the extension of shifting sands. Especially recommendable for this purpose are: *arundo arenaria, clymus arenaria* and other grasses growing upon dunes. These grasses send their roots deeply into the loose soil, consolidate the sand with their roots and rootlets, prevent its drifting and render it, during an undisturbed growth of several years, so compact that trees, which are content with poor soil, may safely be grown there. Common juniper is the tree generally planted to protect that side of the wood area which is principally exposed to strong winds. Other useful trees are the Canadian poplar, some pines as the pitch pine, scrub pine, Scotch pine, some acacias, and even some oaks and birches may be used as an admixture. The leading tree should be the Scotch pine, the planting of which is commonly done by setting out three-year old plants with the balls. If one-year old seedlings are used they should be planted close to the north side of the adjoining sod in order that the sun during the hot summer months cannot so easily penetrate through the soil, and dry up the roots of the young plants.

The most successful attempts for bringing inland sand wastes into such a condition as to use them either as forest-grounds or as grain-bearing fields, have been made in France with the sandy "Landes" of Gascony and of the Gironde. These sand-wastes, containing several millions of acres poor sand land, from one, to one-and-a-half feet deep, with shifting sand at the top and resting upon an impermeable layer of hard-pan, were about forty years ago, during the summer time, great deserts; and during the winter overflown, with water. They could only support a very small population, living on the scant revenue derived from little flocks of poorly fed sheep. At the present time they are covered either with splendid pine and oak forests or with grain-bearing fields. This has been accomplished by first: draining off the stagnant water and then: sowing some of the above-named grasses, the grounds became in due time quite compact. They were then in such a condition that sowing and respectively planting pines in combination with other trees as red oak, post oak, birch and chestnuts could be undertaken. The first two named kinds of trees succeeded especially well; they furnish now the material required by the two provinces for tanning purposes and for cooperage. On some of these lands agriculture is also successfully practiced, but this was only feasible by introducing a rotation in which sylviculture plays a prominent part. The farms are all kept in wood, and after they have thus been brought into a fertile state, a part of the wood is cut down, made areable and cultivated for a period of from 10 to 15 years. The then exhausted area is again planted with forest-trees, and after the lapse of about 12 years again turned over to agriculture. So the inventive genius of modern times has assisted Europe, in repairing the damage done by the nefarious action of improvident and avaricious people, as history shows that four hundred years ago those "Landes" were covered with dense forests, interspersed with many flourishing farms and villages.

With the increasing population of our State and the (alarming) decrease of the principal trees from which tanning material has been hitherto derived, there should the reclaiming of the many millions of barren acres, both in our State and the neighboring States through forest planting not longer be delayed. It is proven beyond any doubt, that tree culture even upon such waste lands as are entirely unadapted to agriculture—see Chapter IV., p. 158;—Chapter precedent—is profitable, and that it is a sure and valuable investment. It is true that landowners will not be inclined to interest themselves in the establishment of high forests and wait from 80 to 100 years for earning the fruits of their labors; and even middle forests, which require a term of from 40 to 50 years for their exploitation, will not be attractive to them, but coppice-cultures with cutting periods of from 12 to 15 years will always, besides improving poor soils, be desirable and well-paying operations. By selecting the proper species among our oaks, acacias, ashes, poplars, willows, etc., it will not be difficult to start a coppice-wood which, will within a term of 10 or 15 years, furnish material not only for the tanner, but also for the cooper and the paper maker.

The *continual* treatment of woods as coppices is not *quite* natural, and cannot be fully maintained, unless the trees to which such repeated exploitations cause death (oaks) are sometimes replaced by seedlings. When for one reason or the other, especially through exhaustion of the soil, these replacements become impracticable, there remains but one remedy, that is to give up the copse culture and substitute for foliaged trees conifers. These will grow well on lands on which the former cannot live, and bring the soil to such a degree of fertility, that it may later be used for agricultural purposes.

CHAPTER IX.

COVERING SAND DUNES ON THE SEA COAST WITH TREES AND SHRUBS.

WHEN the sand in the ocean is washed up by the surf, it dries on the beach and, in this condition, is carried inland by the wind and piled up in hills. The little mineralic grains of which the sand consists, and which, at the surface of the beach, for want of sufficient means to arrest them, are continually in an unsettled condition, will be easily by the winds, brought into a landward motion, covering up, in due time, vast fertile tracts of land with sterile stuff. In Europe, there are made, on several places, the strongest efforts to reclaim millions of acres, which thus had been, from the most fertile fields, converted into sand-wastes. The most remarkable case known is the Tidswilde Hegn (forest) situated at the north coast of the Danish island "Seeland." This island is one of the most fertile spots on the earth, containing a soil which produces the best grain and the finest forests, composed of beeches and oaks. The north coast of the island is exposed to strong winds, which carry enormous masses of sea-sand to the coast, forming there great hillocks. Up to four hundred years ago, forests of foliaged trees extended behind these hillocks, and arrested the flying sand so that the fertile land lying behind the forests were not exposed to the inroads of the sand. But, since then, the woods, which formerly belonged to the Government, came into private hands and were ruined by excessive fellings so that, two hundred years later, the blowing sand had moved several miles inland, covering whole villages and towns with powdered quartz-grains, to the depth of several feet. One hundred and fifty years ago, the Danish Government, in order to protect this beautiful island from complete ruin, commenced operations to confine the shifting sand to the north coast, and to cover its sandy surface with forest-trees. This has been done so successfully that, at present, fine beech and oak forests are grown where, two hundred years ago, several feet of sand were piled up.

However, we need not to go to Europe in order to see the damages done by the shifting sands of the dunes, when the natural protection of the coasts, the forest-growth has disappeared. We have the same spectacle before us on the coasts of Long Island and New Jersey. At the south side of Long Island there were, some thirty years ago, pine forests behind the dunes, which, with the increasing improvements on Coney Island, Rockaway Beach, etc., have been felled. Since that time, the wind commenced to carry the sea-sand into the interior of the island, and now farmers living four miles distant from the coast complain that the sand borne inland by the wind increases from year to year upon their fields, and threatens to bury entire farms in the course of time. To arrest these effects, scientific forestry teaches us, first, to prevent the shifting of the sand on the surface of the dunes; and then to bind the loose soil so as to be able to bear grasses, shrubs and later on, trees. Although the dunes consist of the most infertile and mobile sand, they have the peculiarity of absorbing and retaining, especially in their elevated parts, much humidity; and this peculiarity helps us greatly to control the drifting sand ridges, by covering them with herbaceous and, even with forest-growth, thus permanently binding them.

Among the European nations, there is none that has done more to resist the encroachments of blowing sands, and to reclaim such wastes than France. The arresting and reclaiming of the sand dunes along the Atlantic Ocean, in the Departments of Gascony and Gironde is a work which nowhere has been executed with more skill and success. In consideration of the growing importance of this subject in relation to our State, it may not be out of the way to describe the particulars of this operation a little more minutely.

The operations for arresting the destructive effects of the invasion of the sea-sand consist of (1) the erection of palisades along the coast, by which the dunes situated in the rear are protected from the attacks of the sea-wind and from being exposed to increased sand-drifts and sand deposits ; (2) the work proper, for binding the sand-dunes by aforestation.

1. The magnitude of a performance of this kind renders it necessary to operate in instalments. Usually the place to be worked extends in length from 4,000 to 5,000 feet, and in depth or width about 1,000 feet. In

front of this place a palisade of planks is erected parallel to the shore, about 300 feet distant from the highest water-mark. The planks, from seven to eight feet long, are sunk in the sand to a depth of about 18 inches, a space of one inch being left between them. The sand arrested by the palisade forms, in due time, an artificial dune, sloping towards the sea, with the destination to prevent fresh arrivals of sand from being blown over the place to be cultivated. The sand which passes through the interstices of the palisades, banks up behind them, and strengthens the sand wall. When the palisades, in this way, are nearly covered on both sides, the planks are, with the help of a lever, lifted up, so as to keep them about six feet above the surface, and thus the protection against wind and sand is made *permanent.* Sometimes a fence, made of eight feet long stakes, between which strong but flexible twigs and boughs are interwoven, is substituted for the wooden palisades. As soon as the accumulated sand has nearly reached the top of the fence, the stakes are raised by a lever and interlaced again. These fences, however, are only in less exposed situations employed instead of the planks.

2. Thereupon the place to be worked is enclosed, at the other three sides, by wattled fences. Leaving a space, three yards wide, next to the back fence untouched, owing to the fact that this space will soon be oversanded by the winds blowing from inland and, therefore, unfit for plant vegetation. In distances of ten feet, parallel with the back fence, towards the sea furrows are opened, eighteen inches wide and twelve inches deep, in the midst of which the seed of the maritime pine—a variety of *pinus silvestris*—is drilled and covered with a little sand, mixed with powdered artificial manure. At a distance of eight inches from the middle drill, another drill is made, at each side, in one of which is sown sand-

reed, and in the other furze or gorse. These seeds are also covered with powdered manure and sand, whereupon the *open* furrow is covered with furze or, in want of this, with pfrieme, heather, buckwheat plants, pine boughs or seaweed. The boughs are cut of equal length, about ten feet long, and laid down in rectangular lines to the sea-coast, so that the thick ends of the boughs or plants are placed seaward, and the top of the following bough covers the stem of the preceding like shingles. After the entire area or a part of it is worked and covered in this way, thin but long poles are laid over the ends of the boughs and fastened to the ground with wooden staples, in order to shelter the surface and to keep the movable sand in its place. Under this cover the seeds will germinate and spring up. Wherever should be found steep hill-sides covered with sand-reeds or sand-grasses—a common occurrence near the cavities of the dunes—first of all the plant-growth should be cut down to the root-crowns, otherwise the covering material cannot be distributed evenly over the surface soil when seeding is done; and then the place must be made somewhat level.

The operations of the next year, unless there is intended a lateral extension, are directed to the area parallel with that which has been worked, and is laying behind it. For this section it is only required to erect side fences and a back fence, as the planted section forms a protective wall from the shifting sea-sand. Should there be found some places within the dunes which are compact and solid, *covering* them is dispensed with, and seeding is done in the usual way by drilling in the seeds.

A simpler and, formerly, more frequently employed mode of consolidating the drifting sands upon the dunes is shown in the following:

Fig. I

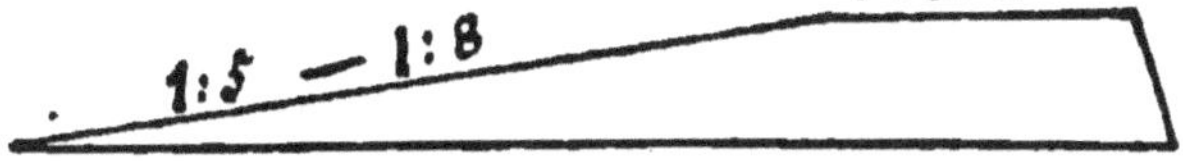

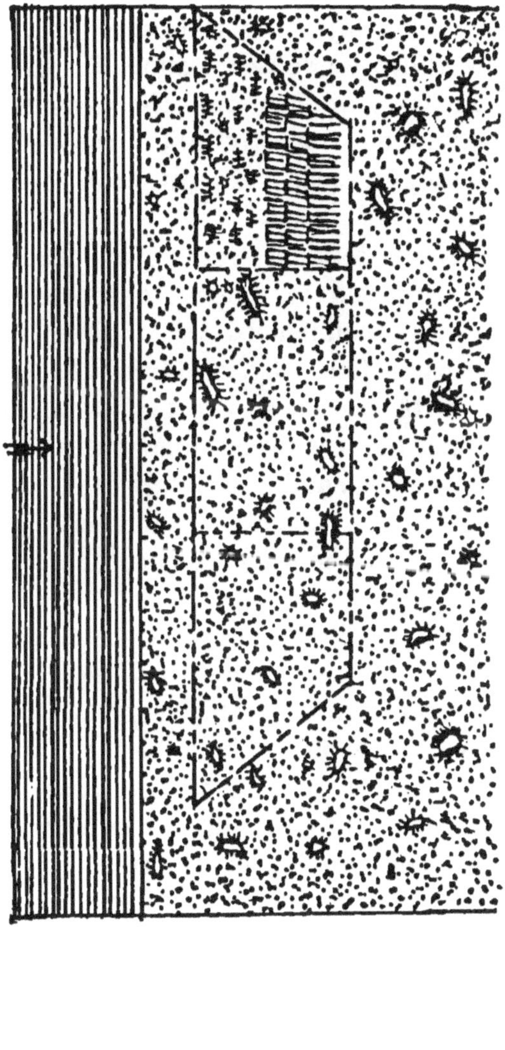

Fig. II

After the place to be worked has been protected in the manner heretofore described, by front, back and side fences and uneven spots, if there be any, leveled, the entire surface is covered with brushwood or small evergreen boughs, about four feet in length; and the seeds of pines, birches, bushes and grasses are sown upon them broadcast. Thereupon the laborers take sand from the adjoining unworked part of the place, and throw at every two feet a shovelful over the brushwood, thus covering not only the seeds, which will, in the meantime, have mostly fallen through the bushes to the ground, but also fastening the loose brushwood to the soil.

This work is done in sections of about three hundred feet long, and of twelve to fourteen feet wide. Generally it is commenced about three yards distant from the back fence by children that, while going backward with the face directed to the back fence, unloosen piles of brushwood, placed in proper distances all over the place, and distribute them over their district, when the seedsman comes to release them. He is then followed by the workingmen, who cover the place with sand.

In the diagram on the opposite page, the formation of an artificial dune is shown by Fig. 1. It begins at the high-water mark of the sea, and gradually rises when the wind is blowing landward, till it has reached the highest pitch at the top of the dunes. If it is desired to hasten this formation, bundles of straw or brushwood, so-called fagots, are stuck into the beach-ground, less in number and height at the start on the shore, and more numerous and taller near the end of the artificial dune.

Fig. 2 shows a fenced-in working place, divided up in three sections. One-half of the first section is finished in the manner described on page 178, the other half is to be worked after the old mode (see page 179), and exposes to view the piles of brushwood set in a circle perpendicularly to the ground, in order that the shifting sands may not cover them.

The maritime pine (*pinus maritima*), which is of such great importance to southern France, cannot be recommended for similar operations in our State, as it requires a warmer climate, such as that of California and the southern Atlantic and Gulf States. If exposed to our dry and cold winds, during the winter, this tree would certainly perish. However, we have among our pines some species which would fully accomplish upon our dunes what the maritime pine has done in France, as, for instance, the Jersey pine (*pinus inops*), the pitch pine (*pinus rigida*), the gray pine or scrub pine, and the red cedar (*juniperus virginianus*). For binding the sand-dunes we have a great selection of grasses and bushes, among which deserve special notice: beach-grass (*calamagrostis arenaria*), myrtle bush (*myrica cerifera*), and such small creeping vines as naturally take root in the movable arid sand of our sea coast.

PART III.

CHAPTER I.

THE OBJECTS OF COVERING MOUNTAINS WITH FOREST-TREES.

THE aforesting of mountains has for its object the creation of a forest vegetation, which should pervade the soil with a net of numerous roots and rootlets in order to bind the soil, especially on the steep slopes, and to prevent its dissolution or sliding down into the valleys by heavy rain storms which underwash the surface soil. The forests of mountains are furthermore destined to furnish to the lower situated, cultivated parts of a country an effective and lasting shelter against meteorological influences, especially against the fury of strong winds. When a tempest beats upon the denuded slopes of a mountain, it will shake the boulders, catch up the stones and overturn isolated trees. These obstacles, far from calming the storm, will redouble its fury; it will rebound and form in the valleys tornadoes which devastate everything that is lying in their way. But when it strikes a wooded slope, each tree, each branch will bend under the force of the wind, but will check its force by its elasticity; the hurricane will be sifted and absorbed by the woods.

But the principal advantage of wooded mountains consists in the furnishing and regulating of a continual flow of water to the lower situated regions. Usually the surface soil of mountains is not very thick and, therefore, unable to retain, for a long time, the quantity of humidity which falls upon it. Mountains that are denuded of forests discharge the mass of melted snow which has been accumulating there during the winter as soon as the warmth of the sun increases in spring. Then the waters and streams rush down the valleys, carrying off whatever they find in their way, swell up the rivulets and rivers of the valleys, into which they flow, and cause enormous damage by the inundations that follow. But when the mountains are covered with trees, the surface soil becomes not only continually richer, owing to the accumulation of leaves under the trees and, therefore, able to support, later on, more and stronger trees, but also thicker, so as to absorb and retain more moisture than the old soil was able to do. During the winter the soil of the forests protected by trees, dead leaves, mosses, etc., seldom freezes, and so the snow under the influence of the warmth of the earth melts so slowly from beneath, that when the warm season appears, sometimes still in the middle of the summer, vestiges of ice and snow can be found there. The consequence of this condition of the ground is that every liquid particle is seized and in its course downward retarded. The former inundations during spring, followed by aridity and low water in the navigable rivers during the summer, cease, and in their stead the discharge of water from the mountains is so regulated as to deliver an equal and continually well-regulated flow. The conclusive proof of these facts is that, in general, abundant springs are almost all situated at the foot of wooded mountains or hills.

In order to obtain with certainty the above-stated objects of sylviculture upon mountains, there should be applied that form of forest management by which the sustained growth of standard (fully developed) trees or high forests will be secured. The so-called coppice management—low forests—by which the reproduction of the trees is done in the natural way of allowing shoots and sprouts to grow up cannot realize the end aimed at, although on many places the condition of the ground will prevent us from raising standard trees in the usual way. In such cases the forester must be satisfied for a long time if he is able to produce a vegetation which will simply improve and respectively increase the soil. Commonly this is done by growing grasses upon the poor grounds, and, when they have increased the mould, bushes may occupy the area, after which planting of forest-trees may be begun, provided the soil has attained sufficient solidity and compactness.

CHAPTER II.

RE-PLANTING FORESTS IN MOUNTAINS.

Selection of Trees—Planting or Seeding.

FOREST vegetation in the plains depends almost exclusively upon the condition of the soil; but in the mountains, besides this, the climate and the formation of the soil play an important part.

By the spontaneous vegetation we perceive at once that with the vertical elevation of the mountains, the temperature of the air gradually is decreasing. This fact proves that there are climatic stations of vegetation, the most downward of which corresponds with the vegetation in the plains on foot of the mountains, while the elevated regions manifestly develop mountainous peculiarities.* In regard to forest vegetation the tree-growing

* It is a well known fact that the average temperature of a locality is decreased in proportion to its distance from the Equator. This principle also holds good in regard to territorial elevations above the sea-level. For we find that each elevation of 300 feet above the sea-level equals, in regard to average temperature, a distance of one degree (65 miles) northward from the Equator.

territory in mountains, therefore, is divided into three stations, viz.:

1. The temperate station or mild region, which *in our State* extends up to about 1,000 feet above sea-level. At this point begins

2. The cool region—middle mountains—and reaches up to about 3,000 feet above sea-level. Thereupon follows

3. The cold region—high mountains—running upward to from 6,000 to 7,000 feet above sea-level.

In the first region regularly grow the same trees which we find in the plains at the foot of the mountains: oak, pine, hickory, black walnut, chestnut, elm, ash, basswood, locust, maple, etc.

The second region produces, under ordinary circumstances, especially the following trees: beach, fir, spruce, hemlock, pine, larch, mountain maple, aspen, willows, etc.

The third region is confined to the crippled and stunted varieties of pine, birches and other hardy trees and shrubs.

But if we will successfully reforest the mountains, we have besides the alleged observation to take into consideration a great many other points, the most important of which we will now briefly discuss.

It is an established fact that trees grown in a higher latitude will easily be raised in a lower region, but not *vice versa;* and that trees of the same zone grow better if planted more hill downward than upward.

Moreover, the elevation of the mountains, the situation of the slopes in regard to wind and sunshine, have great influence upon the growth of trees. The slopes which point to the south and east have a higher average temperature during the year than those which are exposed to the north and west. In following up this natural disposition it is possible to raise, in higher situated regions, trees which are generally found only in lower localities, while on the other hand trees will not grow in their particular region if exposed to more than ordinary hardships, and that in such case—as the forester calls it—the trees "step downward."

Those parts of the mountain slopes which are exposed to the scorching sun rays (south) and the parching winds (west) suffer often by the rapid evaporation of the moisture contained in the soil, and, therefore, do not favor the growth of deciduous trees, but allow only such evergreens as are not so pretentious in this regard, as for instance, pines, cedars and larches.

Sometimes the prevailing winds, being either unusually cold or excessively dry or very wet, change the character of a mountain situation to the worse and do not permit the growth of a vegetation which commonly thrives there; while surrounding higher mountains exercise a protecting effect against such physical influence, and often allow the growth of trees otherwise entirely unknown in such a locality.

The average humidity of the air, in growing forest-trees, should also not be undervalued. So, for instance, the fir, hemlock, spruce, beech, birch, ash and maple, grow better in a more moist air than do pines and even oaks. At all events the effects of excessive warmth upon trees will be considerably counteracted by an excess of moisture in the currents of the air.

The quantity of warmth, light and humidity received by any locality, depends, to a great extent, on the angle with which the sun rays fall upon the same, and therefore the particular inclination of the soil towards the horizon must not be left out of consideration.

While the leaves of the trees feed mostly on the contents of the air, the roots have to draw their support from the soil in which they grow. Therefore, in order that trees may thrive, the quality of the soil, both the mineral and physical, should well be heeded. The mixture of the soil and the proportions in which it contains the principal component parts of the soil, viz., clay, sand and lime is—as every farmer knows—very important. But still more important are the physical conditions of the soil. Very favorable conditions are: depth, friability, moisture and the capacity of the soil for absorbing and retaining warmth and gases. If you find besides these qualities a good humus at the surface, you can be sure to raise the most fastidious trees. Elm, maple and ash require the best soil. Less pretentious are: oak, beech and other nut-bearing trees, the basswood or linden, fir, etc. Still more readily are satisfied: larch, hemlock, spruce, hornbeam, locust, alder, willow, poplar, aspen, cedar, etc., and the least demands are made by the pines and even by some kinds of the birch and alder.

If in selecting the kind of trees, attention is given to these hints, we may be pretty safe to successfully grow forest-trees on a proper place in the mountains. But considering the very great difference which often exists in near-by situated mountain localities, we may still be safer in our selection if we raise those kinds which have grown with success before on that spot or its neighborhood. But even this rule does not always hold good, especially where an area for a long time has been denuded of vegetation and become barren owing to the exposure of the winds and the sun. In such case nature often demands a rotation* in the kinds of trees,

* The doctrine of "rotation" in the culture of forests has been lately very rudely shaken up by theoretical reasons as well as by practical observations. In regard to the former, reference is had to the difference between the growth of grains and that of trees, by which it is claimed that woodlands, through the undisturbed tree-growth, will al-

because the materials of the soil on which the former kinds have subsisted were consumed and the deficiency in the soil had not yet been made up by a natural fallow. The poorer the soil is, and the more unfavorable become other conditions for plant growth, the more difficult is the restoration of denuded mountainous wildernesses. In such case there is no other chance left but to make some judicious trials on a small scale, and if they turn out favorably, to act accordingly.

Planting or Seeding?

The remarks made in Chapter XIV of Part I regarding the question whether we shall *seed* or *plant*, were destined to be applied in the aforestation of tracts situated on the plains. However, they hold in general also good for mountain districts; and as *plantations* are less subject to destructive agencies than *seed beds*, it is the more advisable to give *planting* on mountains the preference to *seeding*, because the peculiar condition of climate, soil and location on mountains impose greater

---

ways be enriched in fertilizing ingredients while the reverse holds true in agriculture, and therefore a rotation of crops, which in a successful farm management, appears to be desirable, can be dispensed with in the renovation of forests. As for the observations made in this direction, the natural rotation in forest-growth is ascribed to natural causes, as, for instance, to the distribution of tree seeds by winds, by animals and even by currents of the waters. However this may be, the fact is undeniable that, provided the soil is equally adapted to both foliaged trees and conifers, the latter grow more luxuriantly after the first have disappeared than when followed by their own kind, and *vice versa*. For the Adirondack forests this question is in a certain respect decided by investigations instituted with old woodmen whose experience, together with that of their ancestors, reaches nearly 150 years back. From these it has appeared that upon the ordinary forest soil 150 years ago, *pinus strobus*, or white pine, was the governing tree, then followed the spruce and lately, foliaged trees such as oak, beech, maple, ash, birch, blackberry, American elm, alder and poplar with intermixture of the hemlock, seem to become leading trees.

hardships upon the plant-vegetation than on plains. For this reason only such seedlings should be selected for mountain plantations as exhibit a strong, vigorous growth, even if they are some years older than those usually transplanted on plains.

Moreover, the peculiar physical condition of mountains, especially the unevenness of the surface and the steepness of the slopes, require, sometimes, alterations in approved modes of forest cultures on plains. So, for instance, when it is decided upon to seed down large sloping tracts with tree seed, there cannot exist much doubt about the direction to be given to the seed-furrows, as it is an unalterable rule in the cultivation of soils on declivities to open furrows only level horizontally. But even the best plowman would not be able to always follow up an exact level direction in transverse plowing. A long continued furrow will soon exhibit irregularities by which, in times of heavy rains, openings will be caused in the furrow through which not only the water, but also washed out seeds and seedlings may be discharged into lower localities. The ruts and grooves thus formed would soon increase in volume and power, and in their further run down hill break through the lower situated seed furrows and destroy many parts of the plantation. For this reason the plowman should, in distances of about 6 feet, interrupt the row after having made openings from 15 to 20 feet long and the next following lower furrow should be so arranged that their openings would face the midst of the unplowed places above. The entire field would then look like this:

```
   20 f.          20 f.          20 f.          20 f.
———————— 6 f. ———————— 6 f. ———————— 6 f. ————————
          20 f.          20 f.          20 f.
       ———————— 6 f. ———————— 6 f. ————————
   20 f.          20 f.          20 f.          20 f.
———————— 6 f. ———————— 6 f. ———————— 6 f. ————————
```

Many alterations of the rules, given for tree-planting on plains, are also, on mountain sites, rendered necessary in the establishment of young plantations. When hardy trees are planted for the purpose of protecting tender ones, the plant-rows have to be run east-westward, in order that the latter ones are protected against the strongest sun rays. But on slopes of mountains there are greater trials in store for young, susceptible trees than sun rays, namely, the danger of being rooted up by heavy rains through the water running downward. To prevent this the plant-rows must always have a transverse direction around the mountain slopes and no attention is given to geographical situation.

CHAPTER III.

RE-STOCKING DENUDED WOODLANDS IN THE MOUNTAINS. —PREPARATORY AND PROTECTIVE MEASURES.

ALTHOUGH, in the restoration of the mountain forests, the selection of the proper kind of trees to be planted is just as difficult as the determination upon the kind of culture, viz., whether we shall plant or sow, far more difficult are the measures we have to take, both in regard to the preparations for beginning the work of cultivation and the protection of the finished work. In localities over which Nature has poured unbounded favors, it is easy to solve this problem and, therefore, we omit such cases, confining ourselves to those which offer uncommon difficulties, and showing how to overcome them.

Nature works with small means to produce great and, to mankind, sometimes very disastrous effects. This is done by the concentration of those little means, and by their joint operation towards the final result. Although man is unable to avert such events entirely, he can lessen their ravages by timely taking up the battle against the single, isolated forces, and thus prevent their dangerous combination. This observation led human genius to the discovery of means and ways to moderate the disastrous effects of violent storms upon the physical condition of mountains, after avarice or imprudence of man had denuded their summits and steep slopes of the forest vegetation, thereby allowing the formation of torrents which carried away the earth, and rendered the restoration of the mountain forests nearly impossible. French engineers and experts in forestry matters have, during the last one hundred years, devoted much time in ascertaining the causes of the origin and dimension of the torrents by which the washing-down of the mountain soil into the valleys and the disastrous, nearly every year, recurring inundations in the mountainous parts of South France were brought about. These investigations led to the following theses, the correctness of which is now fully established:

1. If the mountains are covered with forests, the formation of torrents is impossible.

2. The deforestation of the mountains surrenders the soil to the formation of torrents.

3. By extending the forest area, we do away with torrents, and promote an increased formation of natural water reservoirs.

4. The disappearance of a forest redoubles the vehemence of torrents, and even may resuscitate extinct ones.

We will now consider the various phases in which the accumulated mountain waters may be prevented from doing harm to plant growth, and may even be turned so as to promote forest vegetation.

The Regulation of the Mountain Waters.

It will be remembered that, as a principal requirement for tree-growing in mountains, we have before stated the necessity of procuring and retaining a certain quantity of moisture in the soil. This requirement is the more urgent as the steep inclination of the slopes makes the rain and snow waters run swiftly over the surface without offering them many chances to enter the soil and to percolate it. On the other hand, we see how destructive the waters become if they pour, unchecked, over the slopes, carrying with them vast quantities of earthy components which increase the grinding power of the current, wash the soil from the mountains, and leave bare and sterile rocks behind them. It is in such cases that man's helping hand has to enter the field and to break the steepness of the slopes, the cause of the rapid ruch and destructive power of the waters.

A.—Regulation of Rain and Snow Water on Mountain Slopes.

To break the steepness of the slopes, there have to be dug, horizontally running-trenches or ditches of proper depth and width at appropriate distances, *commencing as near to the top* as is deemed necessary to catch up the waters, making them temporarily stagnant and letting the excess equally flow over the ridge to lower-situated ditches, where the same effects are obtained. This work will be done or, at least, facilitated by a proper sidehill plowing. According to the greater or less steepness of the slope, there have to be made furrows about one foot wide and deep, from six to seven feet apart; or deeper and wider trenches, two feet by eighteen inches, from twelve to fourteen feet apart. The soil taken out of the furrows or trenches is deposited right along the lower edge of the furrow, thus forming a level wall over which the surplus water collected in the furrow or trench will slowly run downward, to be caught up by the next furrow below, unless absorbed by the soil over which it is flowing.

This operation will be a great help for raising trees on steep slopes, by planting them in the middle of the ridges, alongside the trenches. Should the ridges be larger, and have more the shape of a terrace, it is advisable to open in the middle of the terrace, a furrow and plant therein the trees, thus forming an additional obstruction against the waters sweeping down into the lower grounds. The fast-growing root system of the trees and bushes planted upon the mellow ridges will help greatly to strengthen the latter, and thus increase the power of resisting the destructive effects of the water currents.*

Formerly, running down the denuded slope, these waters began to wear out little ruts, then furrows, gulches, channels and, finally, enlarged in width and depth till they became enormous torrents. But treated in the stated way, their force is broken, and they filter quietly into the soil or flow down, impeded by so many obstructions that they cannot do harm. The trenches form also, during the winter, receptacles for the dead leaves of the shrubs and trees and, owing to the half-decayed condition of these leaves, retain, during the

* This mode of cultivation of the soil might sometimes be used advantageously to retrieve the great damages caused to many hilly farms of our State by the improvidence of former owners who stripped the steep hill-sides on the farm of their trees, in order to enlarge the pastures. As such fields usually, by nature, are not rich, and only kept fertile by the shade of the trees grown thereon and by the accumulation of their leaves, they became, when denuded of trees, infertile and barren; whereupon the loose surface soil was washed down by the rain into the lower-situated grounds, covering them with sand and gravel.

spring, the snows cover much longer than the bare soil would do, contributing, in this way, much to the most desirable effect of wooded mountains, viz., the retarded melting of the snow accumulated there during the winter.

B.—Regulation of the Rivulets and Brooks in the Mountains.

Much more difficult is the regulation of the little rivulets, brooks, streamlets, etc., which originate in the mountains, run down in cavities and, uniting with other running waters, form, during heavy rains, torrents which undermine their banks and carry away the best ingredients of the mountain soil into the valleys. In such case, the *first step* to be taken must be to secure the banks of these little waters against the eroding force of the current by planting deep-rooting trees and shrubs upon them as near to the water front as possible. The elm, ash and alder are, on such places, quick growers and will soon be strong enough to protect the banks against further incursions. The *next thing* to be done is to break the force of the downward-running waters by opening furrows at proper distances apart, commencing *as high upward as is necessary*, or by constructing dams or dikes across the beds, grooves or ravines.

With exceptions such as are quite apt to be required by local conditions, the following are the main rules for properly selecting and locating the means of checking the rapidity of mountain waters. Upon a slope of fifteen yards descent in the one hundred (*i. e.*, 15 per cent.) the water flows pretty quietly for fifty yards, then it begins, according to the inequalities and the resistance of the soil, to carry away the earth, showing by this the first point of defense. If the ground is compact, there is not much to fear, but if it is light and exposed towards violent winds, something should be done to avert danger. In this case, however, some transverse furrows would be sufficient for this purpose.

Upon a surface inclined twenty yards in the one hundred (20 per cent.), the water after running about forty yards will begin to loosen the soil and, according to its being more or less compact, the erosion will be more or less rapid. Then low-turfed earth walls should be built strong enough to resist the pressure of the waters, but allowing the flow over the tops without doing harm.

If the slope is one of twenty-five yards to the one hundred, the water after a run of twenty-five yards, digs out ruts and loosens the soil. Then hedges or small fences should be erected to stop the quickened watercourse, and to allow the formation of terraces by the soil and cobble-stones accumulated behind the fences.

When the soil has a slope of thirty yards in the one hundred, it will be dug out by the water after an unchecked flow of twenty yards, and the damming up should begin at this point. With a declivity of forty yards in the one hundred, the unchecked flow of water should not be more than fifteen yards, and upon steeper slopes the establishment of terraces should be more narrowed down.

The diagrams on pages 196 and 197 show the different kinds of dams, dikes and fences which are to be built in order to check the rapid flow of mountain waters. The material to be used depends much upon that which is found in localities where it is to be utilized.

In order to preserve these expensive means, which are both preparatory and protective to tree-growth for all times to come, the terraces created by the accumulation of stones and earth should be consolidated by sowing grasses and planting quick-growing coppice wood.

CROSS-SECTION OF A WOODEN WEIR SECURED BY STONES.

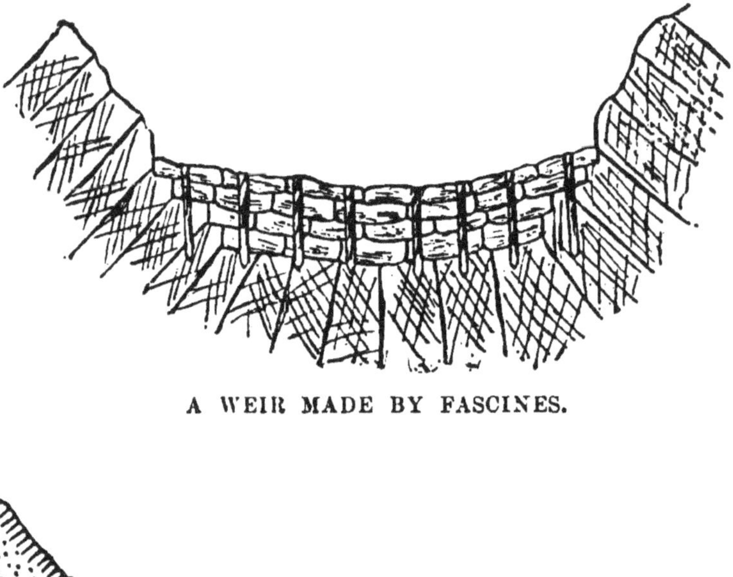

A WEIR MADE BY FASCINES.

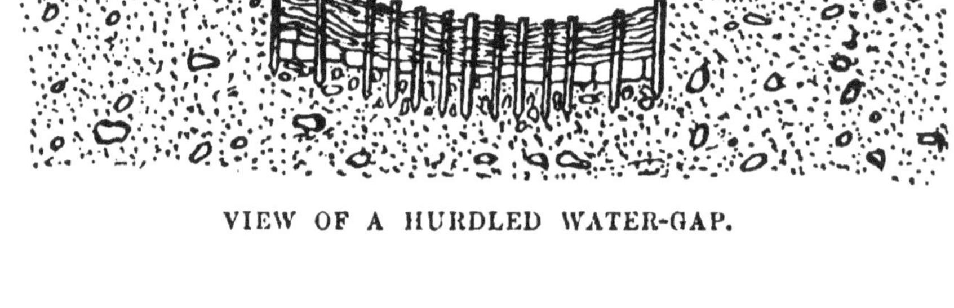

VIEW OF A HURDLED WATER-GAP.

TYPE OF A RUSTIC WEIR OR DAM MADE BY RUBBLE.

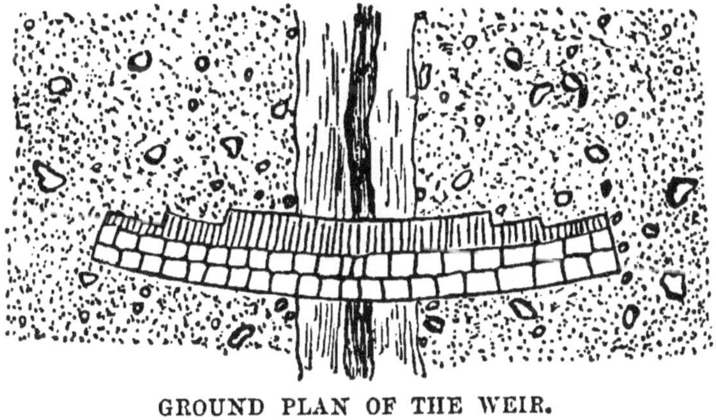

GROUND PLAN OF THE WEIR.

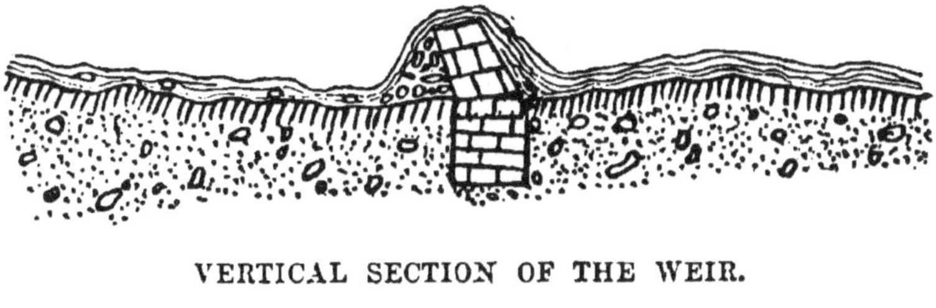

VERTICAL SECTION OF THE WEIR.

When, in the course of time, the soil is increased in quantity and quality, we must endeavor to plant more valuable trees. At all events, upon slopes whose pitch exceeds forty yards descent in the one hundred, the high-forest system is the only rational one, and in stocking with young trees, we should, if the nature of the surface permits, prefer the species having long tap roots, which will bind the soil better.

The proper time to build these dams is, of course, during the season when the waters flow least or not at all. They must be very strong in order to successfully resist the force with which the headwaters, in times, are precipitating themselves into the valleys. It is, therefore, advisable, instead of building a few high dams in great distances from each other, to construct as many as possible low ones. For it is the intention to use these dams not only to obviate the fury of the downward streaming waters, but also to catch up every particle of fertile soil which is being carried below, and thus to make the soil remain in the more elevated parts of the mountains. In order to make the dams strong and lasting, the basis and sides of the same must be protected by fascines, hurdle work or even by rocks and mason work.

This is the way in which the memorable work for restocking the denuded woodlands upon the Alps of Southern France has been achieved, and by which the former frequent and pernicious inundations of the rivers there for the last ten years have been prevented.* It is true the costs have been enormous, but a single inun-

* The best book on this subject is written by the French Over-forest Master Demontzey, who conducted for nearly thirty years the work of re-foresting and returfing denuded woodlands in Algiers and France. The full title of this book is : "*Demontzey F. Traité pratique du reboisement et du gazonnement des montanges. Paris*, 1882."

dation of old would now do more damage than the whole expenses amount to.

After a dam has been perfected, there should be made on both sides outlets in the shape of ditches, having such an inclination as to lead the surplus water, which accumulates before the dam, into transverse running trenches out of which the excess of water flows equally into the territory below.

In regulating the mountain waters we have, however, not only to look out for the very rivulets, streamlets or whatever name may be given to the small running mountain waters, but also for the many *trough-like natural formations of the soil* in the mountains, the ruts, grooves, streaks and even roads, as these in times of heavy and lasting rains often are converted into water currents, quickly changing innocent-looking furrows into brooks and steeply embanked ravines. If possible, these irregularities of the soil must be removed in time, by filling them up with earth, commencing at the highest sites. But if this course is not expedient, there should be constructed at proper places and distances in these cavities crossdams or dikes, capable of arresting flowing waters and leading them through outlets, which are made in the above-described manner on both ends of the dam, into horizontally running furrows or trenches, by which they are scattered over a larger area.

It is advisable to first fill the lower part (bottom) of the large cavities with stones, dead trees and bushes in order to secure drainage under the soil which will there be accumulated as time goes on.

Then commence constructing at the highest part of the ravine in distances from 10 to 50 yards, according to the steepness of the soil, a series of barriers out of fence-wood, fascines or stones. The volume of water at the starting point of the ravine not being large, these barriers will resist the current. Arrested at each instant by these obstacles, the water will deposit there, little by little, some stones, gravel and earth, thus establishing terraces upon which we may plant whatever is required after they have been consolidated on their banks with sods. If such works are simultaneously established in the bed of a ravine there cannot occur any dangerous accumulation of the waters, and they will run down the mountains without violence, feeding springs and fertilizing the fields in the valleys instead of devastating them.

C.—Artificial Irrigation of Mountains Having Very Dry Surface Soil.

The system just alluded to is of great importance for mountains which have a poor, dry soil, particularly for such as contain much lime, because these, owing to their enormous capacity of absorbing moisture, are especially inclined to dry up at their surface. If this system be applied on such soils, it enables to introduce an artificial irrigation by which the greatest results may be expected. For the trough-like formations of the mountain soil will be converted into reservoirs by constructing strong dams across their banks and thus catch up the rain and snow waters. They should have outlets at both ends of the dams from which the water, if wanted, is led off into horizontally-running trenches, over which it will flow slowly and equally, irrigating the area down below. The diagrams (pp.196–7) show how such trenches are built. If there should run off more water than is wanted, the surplus is caught up at a similarly situated lower place, and respectively stored or distributed like that in the higher-lying localities. Treated in this way, whole mountains which would in no otherwise have been made able to produce a green swath, in Europe, have been planted with forest-trees, thereby changing the nature of the country entirely. Formerly, bleak winds swept unresisted over these mountains, drifting away during the winter the snow which sheltered the surface against cold and dryness; and while during the spring, the rains and melting snow rushed over the frozen soil, causing very often, in the rivers of the valleys, inundations which occasioned great losses of life and property, now after a thirty years' wood culture, assisted by the above-described system of accumulating and properly distributing the natural waters over the entire mountain district, the winter snow is all over retained, and when slowly melting, absorbed by a loose and retentive mould; and the rain and snow waters, instead of rushing destructively downward, fill a retentive bed of absorbent soil, storing up a supply of moisture to feed, besides the forest vegetation, perennial springs and brooks.

D.—Regulation of the Overflowing Rivers in the Valleys.

The mountain waters which are not consumed by the soil or air, flow, if regulated as before described, greatly reduced into the valleys, forming brooks and streams or increasing the contents of other streams and rivers. But under extraordinary circumstances there may, in spite of all human precautions, occur such an increase of water that the shallow streams in the valleys cannot hold it but let it run over the cultivated lands. To obviate such overflows, or at least to mitigate their effects, in case they occur, it is advisable to reduce the width of the flowing waters and force them into smaller but *deeper* beds. It is not necessary to make expensive embankments or jetties, the cultivation of the willow—

which we have extensively ventilated on page 148 (Part II.)—alongside the banks is the cheapest and safest means. The natural location of the willow is in low bottom-lands which are exposed to occasional inundations. If planted upon the banks of a river, the willows will thrive and retain, in case of the overflowing river, a great mass of earthy substances enmeshed in its net-work of fibrous roots, after the waters have subsided. At the same time the spongy banklands are made more compact by the luxurious growth of the willow-roots, and able to better resist encroachments caused by the current of the waters.

In the same proportion in which thus the running waters, by the gradual elevation of the banks and their greater consistency are rendered more narrow, the depth of the slanting bed will increase, owing—as every engineer must admit—to the increased force of the narrowed river current. This change produces two very desirable conditions. Firstly, the lands situated behind the willow plantation are protected against inundations by the elevated banks and, secondly, the flow of the deepened and, therefore, largely augmented river is, owing to the decreased slant in the bed, running slowlier, thus contributing *much more* water, during a *longer period* of the year to the receiving river below than the former shallow overflowing rivulet.

If the banks of the rivers in the mountain valleys consist—as is often the case—of gravel, sand and stones carried down by the torrents from the high mountains, the willow cannot be grown on such soil successfully. In that case we select trees and shrubs which are in this respect less exacting in regard to location, as, for instance, the poplar, birch and alder. These will grow, if planted respectively as cuttings or as seedlings, on such soil. If the plantation be well looked after, there will soon, by the dead leaves, be formed a layer upon which will grow mosses and lichens, which, when decayed, under the assistance of the many earthy particles, left by reiterated inundations, help to cover the stony surface in the course of time with such good humus soil as to enable us to raise, later, more valuable forest-trees.

CHAPTER IV.

HOW TO BIND THE SHIFTING SAND ON THE MOUNTAINS.

To bind the shifting sand on the plains and render it compact, adapting it to tree-culture, is a difficult task. But this work is still more difficult when it has to be done in mountainous localities. In the plains we have only to fight the winds, which cause the sand to drift; but in the mountains, besides this, we have to overcome the troubles arising from the unevenness of the soil and its favoring the formation of destructive water currents during rainy weather.

Wherever the sandy soil is sufficiently deep and possesses the necessary components for securing the growth of trees, the work of planting should be at once commenced, this being the only means to prevent the loose sand from drifting, both in the plains and mountains. But when wind and water currents have swept away every bit of soil and vegetation from the slopes, and nothing is left except the rubble-stones, which originated, during past ages, by the corroding action of the glaciers upon the rocky surface, which formed the ground upon which the sand settled, there occur difficulties which appear to be nearly insurmountable. But "forest science" has been brought to bear upon the discovery of appropriate expedients, and found them in some grasses which will grow in such places, producing in due time a cover that will later develop into a sward. If this cover be left for some time undisturbed and not exposed to the attacks of pasturing farm animals, there will appear such beneficial accumulations from above and below the surface that, in the course of time, tree planting may be begun.

The kind of grasses to be principally used for binding the mobile sand and keeping it in its place are : creeping soft grass, tall oat grass, broom grass, tall meadow oat grass, fescue grass, quack grass, wood poa, pimpinella, knotted hair grass, amophila, lyme grass, reed grass or bur-reed. In the lower Alps of France sainfoin has been used for this purpose with great success.

In seeding these grasses the soil, being too mobile, should not be touched either by plow or harrow, and the seeding should be done broadcast by hand, using about twenty pounds of seed to the acre. The only tool to be used in this operation is the hand-rake, for slightly covering the seeds. After the elapse of some years, during which the reclaimed lands should remain entirely undisturbed, there will, through the decay of the old grasses and the spontaneous growth of the young ones, be formed a sward thick enough to allow the raising of some shrubs and arborescent plants, the root system of which qualifying them especially to keep the scanty poor soil together. For this purpose are recommended: juniper, hazel, sallow-thorn or sea-buckthorn, barberry, bladder-senna or bastard-senna, locust or acacia, rosin weed, asp or trembling poplar, white alder, blackthorn, mountain ash, poplar, birch, dwarf mountain and especially the "American" laurel (*Kalmia.*) It has no economic value, however, it is hardy and will maintain a foothold where other shrubs would perish. Its presence has saved in Ulster and Sullivan Counties, N. Y., many a mountain side from the appearance of total denundation.

In order to avoid unnecessary disturbance of the soil, when sowing and cultivating the shrubs and small trees, it is advisable to sow the former together with the grass seed, covering them with the hand-rake, and plant the latter—when one or two years old—three feet distant from each other, in horizontally running rows, six feet apart, using no other tool but the (in Part I.) described short-handled planting axe. Those trees which reproduce themselves from the stumps should, after having grown two or three years, be pruned down so as to leave only a short stump, as by this process the roots will be increased in numbers and strength, and thus the final purpose of the culture of these protective trees will be reached in a comparatively short time.

As soon as the soil has become more compact and the trees in the rows have grown thick enough to afford some protection against the wind and sun rays we can begin planting forest-trees. In selecting these we must pick out those kinds that have strong tap roots, which will run deep into the loose soil and contribute to further strengthen and bind it. To this class of trees belong: oak, pine, fir, larch. They have to be planted, when two or three years old, three feet apart between the above-mentioned (protective) rows by means of the planting-axe. Should the sward be uncommonly thick, there should be dug, at the proper places, plant holes in which to set the trees. In case the sward be very thin, it is advisable to open the plant holes with the hoe, fill them with some good humus soil or compost, and plant therein by hand the trees, putting around them stones or sods as a mulch for keeping the moisture in the soil. But in such case we cannot use trees with large tap roots, we must have recourse to other kinds which form only lateral roots, as, for instance, beech, hornbeam, and particularly spruce hemlock. Should there exist spots, on which no vegetable growth at all is found, they should be left alone, as the time will come when the shade and protection furnished by the surrounding forest vegetation will allow such places to obtain a sward, and then trees may be planted.

At all events, in reclaiming such sandy locations there should, if possible, be avoided any tearing up of the soil, thus leaving a good deal of the work to the kindness and fertilizing power of nature.

CHAPTER V.

RE-PLANTING FORESTS ON MOUNTAINS OF THE SAND-STONE FORMATION.

THE cultivation of the poor sand soil on the plains for farming and even for grazing purposes, meets very often with so many difficulties, that sand-lands mostly are considered worthless. And yet, if they would be planted with suitable forest-trees, both the country and the owner would be benefited, provided the latter is able to stand the expenses of cultivation without expecting any noteworthy income from his property during the first quarter of a century. How easy it is to raise forest-trees on deep sandy soil, shows the cultivation of trees which is effected on mountains of the sandstone formation. With the exception of those parts in these mountains, which are very steep and too much exposed to the sun, and certainly with the exception of such places as are infested with shifting sands, of which we have treated heretofore, there is not much trouble in restoring denuded woodlands on sand-mountains. This formation contains always some clayey component parts and furnishes, if the surface of the rocks becomes more or less dissolved by the air, the best material for creating forests. Usually we find at the top of these mountains a loamy soil, which offers no difficulties for raising forest-trees, unless it is too clayey and, therefore, retains too much moisture. In that case we must resort to the "dam" or "bed" culture, described in a former chapter, and proceed accordingly.

The slopes of the sand-stone mountains commonly contain enough clay to bind the soil, and afford thus every facility to soon re-stock the denuded woodlands thereupon, except the sun and winds have parched the soil, and the natural humidity sunk too deep into the subsoil to be reached by the forest vegetation. In such a case there is no time to lose to stop the loosened sand from running down into the valleys by planting some pines, especially the *pinus silvestris.* This modest and unpretentious friend of the forester is the principal tree which will grow on those neglected places, and render the worn-out soil capable of producing, in later times, more valuable trees.

Although the sand in the valleys of the sand-stone mountains, washed from the slopes, often reaches a considerable height, the spontaneous growth of trees there, dating back perhaps hundreds and thousands of years, shows that this locality is the proper place for the most valuable deciduous trees, viz.: beeches and oaks. Certainly on such sites, if denuded for a long time, and, therefore, having become sterile on the surface, we cannot expect to raise, right away, beeches, as these require besides a friable fertile soil, when young, ample protection against the sun. But the re-foresting can be effected by planting pines in rows, properly distant, and after the pines have reached a height sufficient to overshade and fertilize the surface soil, the interjacent open rows should be planted alternately with beeches, oaks, firs, and larches. It is true that in favorable years and with good seeds, satisfactory results have been obtained by "*sowing*" the last-named trees in the rows protected by the pines; but in general, planting is here also more safe. Planting is easily done by removing the moss from the friable soil and using the short-handled planting axe.

If the soil of the plantation is so poor as to foretell, under all circumstances, a failure in producing foliaged trees, the interjacent rows should be planted with other coniferous trees, especially with spruces, to which should be given a wider position towards each other than is usual with young deciduous trees, viz.: a width of from six to eight feet.

CHAPTER VI.

RE-PLANTING FORESTS ON MOUNTAINS OF THE LIME-STONE FORMATION.

Nowhere is shown the effect of forest-trees upon the soil more convincingly than in the mountains of the limestone formation. The power of the limey or calcareous soil, and its adaptability to promote the growth of forest-trees, are very great and can be enormously increased by uninterruptedly keeping the surface covered with trees. On the other hand, there is no ground quicker deteriorated by being exposed to the sun and weather than the limestone soil. If the ground on the calcareous mountains has been once completely denuded from forest vegetation, there is seldom any hope to stop its progressing sterility. For, on such soil, every moisture received from the air will, owing to the peculiarity of the ground, evaporate much quicker than on any other soil, and the balance of the water will run without any hope of being returned into the depth of the limestone, forming hydrates. Denuded woodlands on limestone mountains, therefore, very soon lose their vegetable mold. At first, it is true, there will spring up a strong sward of grasses; but soon, for want of shade and moisture, the grasses disappear, the soil softens by the rain and snow water, becomes a pap which, after the evaporation of the natural moisture, dries up stone-like, and exhibits at the surface but burned-up spots.

If, on the other hand, forests on limestone mountains are managed so as to have the soil always covered with trees—as is the case with the "planter management"—there will nowhere grow finer beech forests. The cultivation of this majestic tree is natural to this soil, forming the most convenient habitat to the beech. The shade created by the dense growth of the beeches makes the surface soil increase in richness from year to year, and this increase of plant-food furnished by the decaying leaves and twigs of the beech is amply returned to the forest vegetation. Certainly, coniferous trees will succeed on these places just as well as beeches, and as the more valuable kinds of evergreens prove to be commercially more profitable than beeches, the cultivation of the pride of the old European foresters, already diminished by the encroachments made by the agricultural interests in the beech lands on the plains, is in the old country decreasing from year to year.

For the restoration of the denuded woodlands in limestone mountains we have again to resort to the pine, this being the only tree which will, even luxuriantly, grow on such soil.

This observation has led many scientific foresters to assume that pines should be principally raised upon the soil in question. But experience has shown that this was a mistake. The luxuriant growth of the pine does not last longer than the first twenty years of its life;

after that period the pines slowly dwindle away. However, if the growing period be properly used, the restoration of the soil may be so far completed as to begin the cultivation of the beech. With an eye to this object, the plantation of the pines should be considered as a transitory one, and so arranged as to protect the poor soil against the scorching sun-rays, and other attacks made by the elements upon the ground. The larch, if intermixed with pines, has proven a great help for improving the soil, this tree being the only coniferous tree which drops every year its leaves, and thus furnishes more material for the formation of a new humus soil than the evergreens. Under all circumstances the limestone soil may hopefully be considered reclaimed as soon as the pine has gained a foothold upon it. After that, it is easy to plant there beeches and oaks, and other valuable forest-trees.

Should it, for financial or commercial reasons, be considered not advisable to raise pure stock, intermixing pines and larches with beeches can be recommended, as these trees agree very well with each other. But we must avoid to employ here the spruce, on account of its being inclined to encroach upon the growth of neighboring trees. However, we should always bear in mind, that the limestone mountains are the natural home of the beech and, therefore, endeavor to keep, wherever possible pure stock of beeches, this being the only means to increase, by degrees, the fertility of this questionable soil. After the soil having, by continued cultivation of the beech, fully recovered its fertility, it is easy, if wanted, to raise among the beeches other valuable forest-trees, as, for instance, spruce, larch, and ash.

The mode of cultivating trees on limestone mountains is the same as upon sandstone mountains, but the directions given under the chapter of regulating mountain waters and binding the shifting sand should be here very closely observed.

As before stated the pines play the most important part in the reforestation of denuded woodlands on calcareous mountains, and among them the unpretentious Scotch pine usually performs very valuable service. However, in this case the well-known Austrian black pine has proved still more serviceable, it being not only indigenous in high mountains, but thriving also on light, dry calcareous soil no matter how destitute it may be of humus. The foliage of this tree is very thick, and the shade caused by it very dense. The soil, therefore, is supplied with an abundance of detritus, and the humidity, received by the ground from the atmosphere, evaporates but slowly. This pine has no taproot, but sends its creeping roots along the stony ground till they find fissures into which they insinuate themselves, thereby strengthening their adherence to the slippery soil. The cultivation of the Austrian pine offers still less difficulties than that of the Scotch pine. The thin or hardened soil should be torn up by cross-harrowing with an iron harrow, and the seed, about three pounds to the acre, sown broadcast, should be covered by dragging over the field with the brush harrow—see p. 77. If the seed is drilled in, two pounds per acre are sufficient to produce the required density of tree growth, as this pine on account of its thick foliage stands in need of more space than the Scotch pine. In a few years the Austrian black pine will have got itself properly established, putting forth considerable shoots, under the protection of which the beech, as the final stock of tree, may be started. In order to secure a safe and speedy growth of the seedlings the plant-holes on this shallow and stony ground should be well filled with good humus soil or compost.

CHAPTER VII.

RESTOCKING MOUNTAINS HAVING ROCKY SURFACES.

NOTHING can be grown on rocks that are entirely bare except some varieties of mosses and plants of the lowest order which derive their food wholly from the air, and use the rocks only as a holdfast. But, when the surface of the rock has been broken up by the action, both of the rock-devouring bacilli* and the elements—heat and cold principally;—and crumbled into its original composing parts, the growth of plants and trees may take place. This process is still going on all over the earth,

* Very interesting observations in regard to the decomposition of rocky mountains and the formation of humus upon their surface have been lately made by Professor A. Muentz. He found that the continuous dissolution of uncovered rocks was not caused solely by the chemical and mechanical action of the atmosphere; but also in part by some microbes which develop in pure mineral solutions by obtaining the required carbon from the carbonic acid and carbonate of ammonia contained in the atmosphere. These minutest of animalcules penetrate into the smallest, and, to the naked eye, imperceptible fissures of rocks, manifesting their presence by leaving behind them atoms of organic substances which serve to form the first traces of humus. During the winter they rest and take their winter nap; but when the warm season returns, they resume their rock-destroying activity and enter deeper and deeper into the solid stone formation. While the geologist stands here full of admiration at the results of the workings of nearly invisible microscopic creatures, entirely unknown up to the present time; the physiologist is still more astonished at the ability of these bacilli to build up their substance by assimilating carbonic acid and ammonia without the help of any other power but the warmth generated by the oxydation of ammonia. Undoubtedly these microbes have exercised a great influence upon the present contour of our globe, and the accumulation of the plant-nourishing humus; they will continue their action upon the stone formation of our planet till the last rock has crumbled to pieces.

and if we follow the hints pointed out herein by nature we are able to cover rocky surfaces with vegetation much quicker than nature does it herself.

If only a small area with a rocky surface is desired to be planted, the ground should first be covered with sods; and after the turf has become firmly fastened to the rocky foundation, grasses, bushes, and even trees may be grown thereon. But upon bare rocks of larger dimensions this operation would be too expensive and therefore we must look for other means to secure our object.

Regularly the crevices and fissures of rocks, caused by alternate freezing and thawing of the humidity that enters the pores of the rocks, are first filled up with mineralic particles on which plant growth is made possible. These places have first to be taken up and to be planted with suitable shrubs or trees, according to the location and site of the place. The development of the roots of the trees and bushes grown in those crevices helps very much to promote the further disintegration of the rocky surface and the accumulation of ingredients upon which plants and trees feed. As soon as the surface of the rock is sufficiently broken up into small stones, which in time become embedded in some soil, the operation of planting trees can be accelerated by making horizontal terraces at convenient intervals, beginning at the highest point of the place to be improved, and securing the steep edges of the terraces by fascines or wattled willow fences. It will not take a long time ere the spaces between the edges of the terraces become filled up by the further decomposition of the rocks and stones, and then there will be room enough for planting shrubs and trees.

This is the only way in which rocky surfaces of mountainous slopes, on which the mold has been washed down by rain, or been burnt away—as often occurs in the Adirondacks—may be covered with materials for producing a forest vegetation. The terraces may also be secured by planting bushes at their outside, thus forming living hedges. These will in due time be covered by the accumulated earthy substances, and then the decaying vegetation will enrich the soil. Upon the soil, which has accumulated between the edges of the terraces, rows of suitable young trees are set along, which, when properly rooted, will secure the object intended and prevent the recurrence of further damages by keeping the surface soil from shifting.

On rocky steeps where there is little or no visible soil, and where seed can only be deposited in chinks and crevices, or sown in occasional patches of soil, seeding will always have the preference to the mode of planting.

As for the trees and shrubs to be selected for planting in the fissures and interstices of rocks, there are none which serve the purpose of working through their roots upon the rocks better than the Austrian black pine, the ailanthus, crabapple, and the wild rosebush. In regard to the Austrian pine we have seen in the preceding chapter that it prospers even upon the scantiest and poorest soil, and, therefore, is well qualified for the reforestation of bare rocks, provided there are some interstices or fissures into which it can send its strong roots to retain its holdfast. Of the action of the ailanthus in this respect we can convince ourselves easily by looking at some unfinished rocky parts of our great Central Park. There this tree has obtained such a hold upon the rocks that, after the lapse of another quarter of a century, no artificial means will be required to cover those rocks with vegetation. The crabapple and the wild rosebush make so little demand upon the soil that their seeds, fallen into crevices of old brick walls, sprout, grow up, and develop such powerful vegetation in root and trunk that they, in the course of time, tear the walls asunder. The wild roses, besides, have the advantage of sending up many shoots, all around the stem. If these shoots are laid down in from four to five inches deep grooves, and so covered with earth that only the tips are looking above the ground, there will be soon formed such a thick net of rootlets under the surface soil as to bind entirely the soil and keep it together.

Besides the ailanthus French authorities recommend for reforesting localities with rocky surfaces the larch and the pine of Aleppo. The latter thrives upon even the poorest soil, because it draws, like most of the conifers, a large part of its food from the air, increases by its plenty leaves (needles) the soil underneath, and is not affected either by the scorching heat of the sun or the blasting winter winds.

These trees and shrubs permit even grasses to grow under their shade, and thus aid to increase the mold on the rocky surface by the successive growth and decay of the vegetation, enabling us, as time goes on, to plant more valuable trees.

It happens very often that the soil upon the said terraces is neither sufficiently thick nor stable enough to furnish a good bed to the young trees. They grow there very slowly and poorly, their roots being unable to hold on the little soil which should cover them, but is washed away by rain, so that the roots receive their subsistence only by the humidity retained on the overlaying stones. In such cases we have to sow quickly and vigorously growing fodder grasses, either before planting or shortly afterwards, as these at first give the best protection for young trees against meteorological influences; and later, when decayed by the shade of the growing trees, they increase the fertile soil. At all events, these grasses prevent the washing away of the thin soil by rain storms.

The French have had a long and satisfactory experience in this matter, as they have during the past thirty years undertaken the reforesting of the denuded wood and grass lands on the Lower Alps. They recommend principally the esparsette, as giving the best protection to the saplings. But as this grass runs out after three or four years, unless resown, it is, when the plantation requires protection during a longer time, usually mixed with other grasses, especially with *bromus erectus, avena elatior, holcus mollis, lasiagrostis, calamagrostis,* and pimpinella. Mixing is done in the proportion of seventy-five esparsette to twenty-five of the bulk of the other grasses. It is true that the admixed grasses do not fully develop until two or three years after being sown, but they last much longer than the esparsette.

CHAPTER VIII.

RESTOCKING DENUDED WOODLANDS ON HIGH MOUNTAINS.

THE attempts to repair the damages caused by the cupidity and imprudence of men to the woodlands on those mountains which extend upward to from five thousand to nine thousand feet above sea level, have shown how hazardous it is to interfere, however slightly, with whatever nature has arranged by the work of time. The high mountains are the principal sources and headwaters for navigable rivers. Whatever tree, bush or shrub may grow there forms a protection against uncommon flowing off of the water supply, and, therefore, should never be touched, the penalty for the violation of this rule being often an irreparable injury to the best interests of the commonwealth. European countries have enormously suffered from the reckless devastations committed on the high mountains during the last two centuries. Southern France above all labored heavily under the inundations caused every year by the torrents pouring down unchecked from the denuded mountains. But the great efforts both financial and scientific, made by France during the last twenty-five years, have culminated in a success, of which that nation can justly be proud. While France thus has been expiating a great politico-economical sin of former generations, that part of Austria-Hungary, which surrounds the Adriatic Gulf, and contains a territory of about four thousand square miles, is now threatened with entire sterility by shifting sands, unless the exertions initiated recently for reforesting the denuded woodlands on the high mountains of the coast meet with success. In a short time men can destroy through ignorance and avarice what took nature centuries to build up. If the summits and higher parts of the mountains be entirely denuded, the force of the winds, being there nearly irresistible, checks the growth even of those grasses and sedges which usually spring up there luxuriantly, when not disturbed or tied down by the elements.

In order to restock the denuded woodlands on the high mountains, there should, in the first place, be strictly observed the directions heretofore given in regard to the regulation of the mountain waters and springs and to the binding of shifting sands, as far as applicable to the requirements of the locality. But the greatest hindrances to be fought against here are the high and destructive winds which prevent the growing of any forest vegetation on these exposed regions. To obviate this evil, the first thing to be done is to cultivate the coarser kind of mountain grasses to act as a protection to the future plantations. After a few years' undisturbed growth, during which the grasses have been protecting the ground against the damaging influence of cold, dry, and stormy weather, we can commence planting in rows from twelve to fifteen feet apart shrubs and bushes of the hardiest kind, such as juniper, sorbtree, common hawthorn, etc., as a protection to subsequent plantations. As soon as they have gained a good hold upon the soil, the intervening, empty stretches should be filled with additional protective rows, containing, according to climatic circumstances, pines, larches, wild or dwarf pine, grey alder, birch, willows, aspen-trees, etc.; while the spruce, the fir-leaved pine and sometimes larch and wild mountain pine should be planted later for forming the stock of trees. Among the pines there is no species which serves better the purpose of re-stocking steep and high mountain plateaus than the oft-mentioned Austrian black pine. It gets along well on declivities and high situations, and all exposures seem to agree with it.

Should pines grow well—a case which seldom occurs in these high regions—it is advisable to plant the entire area with pines as the stock of trees. After they have fairly developed, open spaces found between them should be filled in with spruces.

But should the growth of the spruce prove satisfactory for forming the stock of trees, larches are to be used as a protection, and should be planted in rows from twelve to fifteen feet distant, to serve as a windbreak to the spruces which will later be planted in the alternating open spaces. For the spruce being one of the hardiest trees, is able to live farthest up on the mountains, and, therefore, is especially qualified to form the stock of trees in the higher regions.

Should it be practicable to successfully grow the larch, then the wild or dwarf mountain pine (*pinus pumilio*) may be used as a covering and protection to the former, during the first period of its growth.

In the very highest regions, there does not exist any forest vegetation except the wild or dwarf mountain pine; to try other trees is sheer waste of time and money.

Finally it should always be borne in mind that in undertaking to replant such exposed localities, the operation never should be begun at a place which is from all sides exposed to the inclemencies of the weather and situation; but work must, if practicable, be commenced at a place which adjoins an existing stock or clump of trees or has any other protection, and, shielded in this manner, planting should gradually go on till the whole area is set out.

The seedlings to be employed in bleak and exposed situations should be brought up as hardy as possible, and so that they take girth in proportion to their height and develop such a strong root system as to hold them firm against violent winds. For this reason, when large tracts in those locations are to be reforested, there should be established in the midst of the grounds a nursery for raising the required seedlings because plants grown under less trying circumstances would not thrive here. Certainly the nursery must be sheltered against severe winds by building substantial stone walls or earth embankments around them. These dams should not be higher than about six feet, but they should be covered with a strong and projecting coping by which the wind is broken when it rises at the wall. If the seedlings in exposed localities are too much sheltered, they are unable to withstand the severity of the exposure when transplanted to their place of destination.

As to the expenses of the operations, it is well known that they are very heavy, because most of the work has to be done by manual labor and a return, if at all, will come in very late and very slowly. Therefore it is no wonder that private property situated upon high mountains, after it has been stripped of the trees, is abandoned by the owners and left to the care of the government. Such property never should go into private hands, but always ought to be retained by the government. The latter have the means to undertake the expensive cultures called for by an urgent politico-economical necessity, and need not expect any other return from the amelioration than that which results to the general welfare of the people.* Besides, governments have always thousands of strong hands at their disposal in the public prisons. They cannot make better use of them, both for the prisoners' own sake and that of the commonwealth, than to employ them in this kind of work.

The State of New York would undoubtedly derive a great benefit by adopting some such measure, and going on to replant the denuded woodlands in the Adirondacks, whereby it would be self-evident that the State should be the owner of the high mountain territory. At the same time the State would solve in the most simple way the grave question of competition of prison labor with free labor. There was some time ago a report in the newspapers about a visit paid by Governor Hill to the Clinton State Prison which, as is known, lies in the northwestern part of the Adirondacks, 1,700 feet above sea-level. In this report it was stated: "*that there*

---

* See the remarks on pages 24 and 25.

were 500 *convicts kept busy every day, each of them being worth* 50 *cents a day to the State. The State made garments and overcoats at prices from* $3.50 *to* $6.00, *which could not be produced from any tailor in New York City under* $12 *or* $15." Now would the public interests of the State of New York not much better be promoted if these prisoners were kept busy in replanting and improving the denuded woodlands in the Adirondacks; even if they were then worth much less than fifty cents a day to the State, than to compete with the cheap tailoring in our cities?

CHAPTER IX.

CONCLUDING REMARKS.

State Forest Nursery—Forest School—Forest Experiment Station—Asylum for the Game.

THE preceding chapter brings us to the end of the discussions outlined in the preface, in which, when written some time ago, the application of scientific forestry to our State forests was considered more as a possibility for the future than in the expectation that the principles which it advocated were so soon to be realized. But as a great and significant change in public sentiment, leaning toward the author's views has taken place since that time, a few further remarks may not be out of place.

The Forestry Act of 1885 provided in fact solely for the protection of the State forests against fire and thefts, but made no attempt to have them managed efficiently. The Adirondack Park Association, however, as stated on page 139, has taken the matter in hand, and is endeavoring not only to bring about an enlargement of the State property in the Adirondacks in order to secure the water sheds of our navigable rivers against further wanton wood destruction; but also to introduce a systematic management of the State forests with the view of making them a source of permanent revenue for the State.

Now the question arises whether this change of policy by which the State appears as a great landed proprietor and dealer in wood products is desirable in the face of the strongly existing American idea that the Government never shall compete with private industries and occupations, but must only interfere to secure perfect freedom of labor and facilitate private enterprise.

And here we may, without resorting to the dangerous expedient of forming new schools of economists for America,* on general grounds as well as by the experience of other countries enjoying the same free institutions which we possess (*e. g.* Switzerland), answer this question unhesitatingly in the affirmative.

The Adirondack region as a whole is, with the exception of lands situated along the river valleys and the shores of some of the larger lakes, utterly unfit for agricultural purposes. As soon as the timber is taken away the owner of the tract has no more interest in it. Seeding and harvesting time are too far apart from each other. The forest-planter will never reap the full benefit of his labors, and therefore, the owner does not feel like going on to replant a tract which he has just stripped of its trees to realize the anticipated benefits of his property. To replant his denuded lands a large capi-

* See "Annual Report of the Division of Forestry for 1887," p. 47, init.

tal is required, and this capital will be tied up for generations, and pay only at the end of a long period accumulated interest together with the invested money. This kind of business does not agree with the average American. He prefers to have his capital at his disposal and when he uses it, he expects to make high profits and quick returns. To the State, however, the material value of the wood products are of secondary significance; the economic influence of those wooded mountains upon the general weal of the country is the principal reason for endeavoring to obtain control over a region which will secure the ascribed economic effects only when continually kept under wood.

And yet there are some peculiar features about the possession of well-managed forests which should make them extremely desirable for the many rich people we have in this country, and who can afford to tie up a part of their wealth for a longer period before receiving returns. These features are:

1. The investment is as safe as in the most solid savings bank, and at a rate of interest which at least equals that paid by the banks.

To prove this, is not difficult, but it would lead us here too far to do it. Suffice it to observe that the closest calculations made in European countries in regard to wood accretion in the forests confirm the correctness of this statement, which will be still more applicable to our country as the growth of trees here by far surpasses that in Europe, and the rate of interest is the same in both countries.

As for the much-feared forest fires, it is to be hoped that we also will be able to discover and apply some such means, both of preventing and extinguishing forest fires as have been devised in Europe so that there at present any danger of passing railroad trains through wooded districts has been removed.

2. The labor required in the management of forests is much smaller than that employed in any other business, especially in the allied one, of agriculture; but any sum of money properly spent in the administration and exploitation of forests will always give sure and highly satisfactory returns. See pp. 17 and 18.

3. Forest lands are bound to be in the future much more high-priced and remunerative than they are at present, because with the continually increasing population in our State and country the demand for wood products will become larger and influence their prices to such a degree as we are now unable to imagine. The first importation of foreign pine will send up the price of American pine to the cost of production.

Considered solely from a business standpoint, the said features would render the possession of forests greatly acceptable to corporations and governments, as these are supposed to be not confined to the short natural term of human life, and, therefore, will live to enjoy the full benefits to be derived from forest planting and forest management. To our State the acquisition of the Adirondack forests would be the more desirable *as this is the only means to preserve the wooded condition of that region* for the purposes for which they are by a benign Providence destined, viz., to protect and benefit the country in its physical condition, and to furnish a permanent supply of lumber, timber, and fuel. It is true, there has been in p. 13 expressed a somewhat different opinion in this regard. But those lines were penned under the impression that the imperfect views about "forest preservation," laid down in the Forestry Act of 1885 would not so soon be given up, and substituted by sound business principles—and under those circumstances every enlargement of the State forest preserve would have only increased the public expenditure, without even attaining the object of the "*preservation*" of the State forests.

This state of things has been lately changed altogether, as the Adirondack Park Association has made the introduction of a systematic, paying management of our State forests the condition under which the acquisition of the Adirondack Park grounds is to be effected. This is the only correct and expedient step to be taken in the matter. *For without proper management the protection of woods from their many foes, both human and elemental, cannot be realized.* But with a rational management we can not only effect the fullest preservation of the Adirondack forests but we will also lay the foundation for a future revenue which will in the course of time not only blot out the capital invested in the acquisition and the management of the forests, but also create a source upon which the people may draw for helping to defray the public expenses.

As the projected enlargement of the State forest domain and the preparatory measures necessary for the introduction of systematic forest culture involve a large amount of money and labor, it is but just that a considerable number of intelligent and public-spirited citizens should be enrolled to fulfill a patriotic duty in which they themselves have not only to lay aside every shadow of partisan spirit but also to secure by proper legislation the adoption of such principles and rules for the future organization and management that mere political influences will never be permitted to interfere with the technical management. If we ever shall enjoy the benefits justly expected from the projected public acquisition, we have to subject the entire institution to some such rigid civil service rules as exist in the Metropolitan Fire Department or Police Department of the City of New York. Without such unalterable restrictions the management of the State Forests would soon become the most coveted ground for political spoil-hunters, and the State, instead of expecting an income, would soon find its hoped-for revenues crumble down so as to leave only from year to year increasing expenses of management.

It is only to be regretted that the said association has thought proper to assume the name of a "Park" association because this leads to misunderstandings which, as experience shows, may prove injurious to the project by provoking the opposition of our rural legislators. In a correspondence which the author directed to the *New York Times*, Feb. 27, 1890, it was stated that our country population regarded the project of a forest park in the sense that its aim was the maintaining of woodlands as a shelter for game, and as a region of pleasure resort for those who can afford time and means for this enjoyment. For this reason even the harmless provisions made for the preservation of the State forests in the Forestry Act of 1885 experienced a strong opposition in the Legislature, although no considerable grant was demanded, because the opponents of this measure represented to the masses that such parks were but resorts for rich people, and that no regular exploitation of the woods and no felling of trees would take place; and that, therefore, the growth of timber for the supply of man would come to an end, turning out very disastrous to the local population that mostly were subsisting on the products of the woods.

That this apprehension was well founded shows a

correspondence from Lockport of this State, where lately a farmers' meeting was held in which the idea of establishing a public park in the Adirondacks was discussed, and finally very violently opposed. Manifestly, the old foes to the preservation of our State forests, who operated also against the tame Forestry Act of 1885, were there at work, and blinded the unsuspecting rural population by the linguistic definitions of the word "Park." The *N. Y. Times* made to this meeting the following very appropriate remarks:

"There evidently was a serious misunderstanding of the nature of the case which calls for explanation of this desirable project. This (park) is not for private uses and for the enjoyment of a few wealthy persons who may spend their leisure weeks of annual vacation there. It is for the public advantage; for the preservation and profitable use of a valuable store of timber; for the preservation and supply of the water which maintains great and indispensable channels for commerce which have built up the Empire State, and upon which the continued prosperity of the State depends, and also for the favorable effect upon the climate of the vicinity, broadly extended, of a great source of rain."

However, when the projected enlargement of the State forests is secured, and the management shall begin operations in a business-like way, we will find that we need a large tract of woodland, which has to be treated somewhat differently from the general forest preserve, and this tract should be distinguished from the preserve by naming it the "Park."

This park should, among other purposes, be devoted :

I. To the establishment of a State nursery for forest trees.

The proper preservation of natural forests requires,

besides other operations, the continual care for replanting areas which have been denuded either by accidents (fire) or elemental forces (storms, snow) or by the natural course of tree life. Of the present State forest preserve there are several hundred thousands of acres of woodlands, which have been stripped in such a manner that they forever are doomed to weeds and brambles unless the helping hand of man is enlisted into service for restocking them. Many of these tracts may be reforested by a general cultivation and seeding down with the seeds of trees adapted to soil and location, but there will remain many places which cannot be redeemed from their desolate condition unless planted with seedlings, and sometimes with such ones as have been once transplanted in the nursery. It is true that wherever large tracts are to be planted the nursery should be located in the midst, or at least near the tract to be operated on. But this would not exclude the advisability of creating a principal station for general nursery purposes. For this institute has not only the care of raising seedlings and disseminating the knowledge of improved methods of forest planting, but also of collecting the seeds of forest trees grown in the Adirondacks, and of preserving the collected seeds till the time arrives when they will be made use of. Sometimes it may not be avoidable to buy tree seed from seed-dealers. But it goes without saying that, to owners of large forests, the most approved way of restocking their denuded wood plots is to take the collection of seeds in their own hands, although this operation is a tedious one, and not infrequently more expensive than to buy the seed from the dealers.

II. *A Forest School* would be another institution to be established upon the privileged grounds of a *Forest Park.*

With the introduction of systematic forestry men trained in all branches of forest planting, and in the protection and exploitation of forests will be required in great numbers. Referring to what has been said on this subject in Chapter V., Part I., the following remarks may serve to give some more useful hints in this regard.

For the proper management of large forests there are required two classes of officials, besides common laborers, viz.: 1. The persons of the forest administration service occupying the higher places in the department, supervising the entire business and giving directions to the local officials in the forest service for the suitable methods of cultivating and exploiting the several wooded tracts entrusted to the care of subordinate officials as foresters and their assistants. 2. These subordinate officials, although occupying the inferior places in the service, are with us in the present transitory stage of converting the wild woods into cultivated forests of the highest importance, because the principal work during the first years will, besides the engineers' work of laying out and rendering passable the necessary roads through the woods, consist of cleaning and clearing out the thickets, felling off mature and overmature trees, removing them out of the woods and preparing them for the auction sale and the market, putting the denuded woodlands in the proper condition for the reception of seeds or plants, and reforesting them.

With the further development of the profession, to be built up by introducing scientific forestry in this State and country, there will undoubtedly appear forest officials of the class No. 1, who have received besides practical instruction in the culture and management of forests, an university education to fit them for the forest administration service, and to apply their widened knowledge and experience for the benefit of the State by increasing the revenues of the forests entrusted to their care. But, at present, we need, *par excellence,* men of class 2, practically instructed in the everyday routine of systematic forest management, after having received the education of the average graduate from a *country school.* To impart such an education and to accustom the students to a strict moral conduct and a rigid, nearly military discipline, without which no large forest can be managed successfully, the immediate establishment of a *forest school* within the Adirondack Park should be insisted upon. There young men between 18 and 22 years old should receive an elementary education and practical instruction under the direction of an approved forester.* This school should be located at a place where the teacher, for purposes of practical instruction, can have at his disposition an extended area consisting of standing wood, denuded woodlands, and a well-equipped nursery. The students should be compelled to devote half of the time of their education for performing every manual work that is required to be done in the proper management and exploitation of forests. Referring as for the rest to what has been said in this regard on page 33, *sqq.*, it might not be amiss to remember the experiences we have made with our agricultural schools† and not to raise in this school the

---

* We need not to fear a want of scientifically educated foresters. The reverse might come nearer to the truth. See what is said about this subject on page 142, note.

† The last report of the Cornell University goes to show that, out of a total number of 1,300 students, only thirty-one are inscribed in the Agricultural Department. "This meagre showing is," as the *Practical Farmer* lately said, "not the result of poor or unqualified professors

standard of professional education higher than is necessary for the executive staff of the forest department. However, should there be found talented scholars with higher aspirations, occasion should be given to them after completing the full course in this school to enter a college for obtaining a higher standard of education to fit them for the higher walks of the profession.

III. The State Park should also afford an opportunity for creating an experiment station for forest trees.

Our knowledge of *where, what,* and *how* to plant trees is, as the late Dr. John Warder said, very imperfect. There are only two ways to complete this knowledge, viz., either by experience or by experiment. In Europe it took more than a century to organize a system of scientific forestry, and since that time the experiment stations are fully engaged in disclosing the many dark points which remain in this science still doubtful, in spite of the excellent management of the European forests by erudite and capable men. Now, if we intro-

---

and instructors, for they are the best that can be found. The trouble lies in the system. There is a natural antagonism between agricultural and classical students, and they will never in any manner coalesce; the former being in the minority, the latter will drive them by sneers and taunts either into a strictly literary course, or send them home in disgust." What should be done and can be done to avoid such undesirable condition may be seen in the little "Storrs Agricultural School" of Connecticut. This is a purely agricultural school, costing but a few thousand dollars every year, and has many more students than the Cornell University has in its agricultural department. The graduates of this school go all back to the plow and realize practically the benefits of their education, while *most* of the *few* graduates from the Cornell agricultural department enter city and business life. Let us have a little forest school in the Adirondacks for educating the men required to perform the practical operations in the management of the State forests. Cornell University may rise to educate the higher officials who, later on, will be in demand for the administration of our State forests, and who should possess an university education.

duce a systematic management of our forests with helpers who are nearly all crude lay hands, it devolves upon us the more the duty of establishing experiment stations as the objects of our investigations are by far more numerous and complicated than those treated in the European stations. The principles of vegetable growth being everywhere alike, we can obtain much useful information by the instructions of the European foresters. But as our climate and physical conditions differ much from those prevailing upon the Eastern hemisphere, and as these circumstances effect different results in forest culture, we have to make careful observations and experiments ourselves, in order to arrive at the knowledge necessary to determine the most important steps in the rational management of forests. See the remarks on page 53 i. f.

An experiment station in the Adirondack Park would be the more beneficial for the whole country, as we would be able to attach to it a large tract of woodland and an extensive nursery, thus combining the experiments in the forest with those in the field (nursery). We would be able in the course of time, by careful measurements of trees, to determine: the rates of growth in different species of trees, at different periods of life, and could answer the question whether it would pay to devote a certain area to forest culture.

We could furthermore determine the technical and financial value of the different species, their wood accretions under different conditions, and at a certain age, and would then be in a position to decide on the most desirable selection of trees from a financial point of view. We could then answer many questions which are at present still entirely wrapped up in darkness, or very doubtful, such as regarding the conditions under which the different kinds of trees grow best and form the most wood, some requiring close and some more open planting, some needing nurses and some not, some requiring much light, while others get along well in the shade. All these points, and many others connected with the various forest cultures in seeding and planting forest trees, which are so important for the systematic management of forests and not yet settled, should be attended to and by experiments determined, with the help of tentative processes.

IV. The Park idea would, however, be still more appropriate if it was made subservient to another economic consideration, viz., to the preservation of the game within the Adirondack region. Under the present system of administration pot-hunting in the Adirondacks will, from year to year increase; and, unless there is set apart an extended district where game may rest and breed undisturbed, the nobler species of game will soon be a thing of the past. It was only by declaring some of her mountains (Freiberge) exempted from the incursions of hunters and trappers that Switzerland succeeded in saving the beautiful chamois from total extinction. If we take similar precautions and set apart a large continuous wooded tract as a park, we could establish it at the same time as an asylum for the much-persecuted game, in which hunting and trapping game should be prohibited under the heaviest penalties. Then we *would* not only preserve a stock of the pretty game for our successors without being compelled to keep a costly deer park, we would at the same time protect people who visit the park for pleasure or health against the sinister stray shots of the pot-hunters to which visitors of the Adirondacks are now exposed at all times and in all places.

A list of native trees of New York, published in the last Annual Report of the State Forest Commission, is as follows. Those marked with an asterisk being within the boundaries of the projected Adirondack Park :

Willow or peach-leaved oak.
Black Jack or barren oak.
*Black or yellow-bark oak.
Scarlet oak.
*Red oak.
Pin or swamp Spanish oak.
Post or box white oak.
Over-cup white or bur oak.
Mossy-cup oak.
White oak.
Swamp white oak.
Rock chestnut oak.
Chestnut or yellow oak.
Shellbark or shagbark hickory.
Mockernut or whiteheart hickory.
Pignut or brown hickory.
Bitternut or swamp hickory
*Sugar maple or hard maple.
*Black sugar maple.
*Soft or swamp maple.
*White or silver maple.
Ash-leaved maple or box elder.
*White birch.
*Canoe or paper birch.
*Yellow birch.
*Black or cherry birch.
*Red birch.
*Red beech.
*White ash.
*Black ash.
Green ash.
*White elm.
Slippery or red elm.
Cork elm or Thomas's elm.
*Quaking aspen or small poplar.
*American aspen or poplar.
*Virginia or necklace poplar.
Cottonwood or downy poplar.
*Balsam poplar or tacmahac.
*Balm-of-Gilead.
Chestnut.
Horse chestnut.
*Black willow.
Yellow willow.
Black walnut.
Butternut.
Locust.
Honey locust.
*Black or wild cherry.
Sweet gum or liquidambar.
Buttonwood or sycamore.
Persimmon.
Pepperidge or sour gum.
Nettle tree or hackberry.
Red mulberry.
White mulberry.
Kentucky coffee tree.
Magnolia or cucumber.
*Basswood or linden.
Tulip tree or whitewood.
*Ironwood or hop hornbeam.
*Hornbeam or water beech.
*Flowering dogwood.
Dogwood.
Judas tree.
Holly.
Sassafras.
*Black thorn.
*Mountain ash or rowan tree.
Sweet-scented crab.
Sheepberry.
*Stag-horn sumach.
*Wild red or pin cherry.
*White or Weymouth pine.
*Pitch pine.
*Yellow pine.
*Scrub pine.
*Black or double spruce.
*White or single spruce.
*Balsam or balsam fir.
*Hemlock.
*Tamarack or hackmatack, or larch.
*Red cedar.
White cedar.
*Arbor vitæ or white cedar.

INDEX.

Mushrooms. How to Grow Them.

For home use fresh Mushrooms are a delicious, highly nutritious and wholesome delicacy; and for market they are less bulky than eggs, and, when properly handled, no crop is more remunerative. Anyone who has an ordinary house cellar, woodshed, or barn can grow Mushrooms. This is the most practical work on the subject ever written, and the only book on growing Mushrooms ever published in America. The whole subject is treated in detail, minutely and plainly, as only a practical man, actively engaged in Mushroom growing, can handle it. The author describes how he himself grows Mushrooms, and how they are grown for profit by the leading market gardeners, and for home use by the most successful private growers. The book is amply and pointedly illustrated, with engravings drawn from nature expressly for this work. By Wm. Falconer. Is nicely printed and bound in cloth. Price, post-paid........ 1.50

Allen's New American Farm Book.

The very best work on the subject; comprising all that can be condensed into an available volume. Originally by Richard L. Allen. Revised and greatly enlarged by Lewis F. Allen. Cloth, 12mo... 2.50

Henderson's Gardening for Profit.

By Peter Henderson. New edition. Entirely rewritten and greatly enlarged. The standard work on Market and Family Gardening. The successful experience of the author for more than thirty years, and his willingness to tell, as he does in this work, the secret of his success for the benefit of others, enables him to give most valuable information. The book is profusely illustrated. Cloth, 12mo... 2.00

Fuller's Practical Forestry.

A Treatise on the Propagation, Planting, and Cultivation, with a description and the botanical and proper names of all the indigenous trees of the United States, both Evergreen and Deciduous, with Notes on a large number of the most valuable Exotic Species. By Andrew S. Fuller, author of "Grape Culturist," "Small Fruit Culturist," etc. 1.50

The Dairyman's Manual.

By Henry Stewart, author of "The Shepherd's Manual," "Irrigation," etc. A useful and practical work by a writer who is well known as thoroughly familiar with the subject of which he writes. Cloth, 12mo........ 2.00

Truck Farming at the South.

A work giving the experience of a successful grower of vegetables or "grain truck" for Northern markets. Essential to any one who contemplates entering this promising field of Agriculture. By A. Oemler, of Georgia. Illustrated. Cloth, 12mo........ 1.50

Harris on the Pig.

New edition. Revised and enlarged by the author. The points of the various English and American breeds are thoroughly discussed, and the great advantage of using thoroughbred males clearly shown. The work is equally valuable to the farmer who keeps but few pigs, and to the breeder on an extensive scale. By Joseph Harris. Illustrated. Cloth, 12mo........ 1.50

Jones's Peanut Plant—Its Cultivation and Uses.

A practical Book, instructing the beginner how to raise good crops of Peanuts. By B. W. Jones, Surry Co., Va. Paper Cover,.... .50

Barry's Fruit Garden.

By P. Barry. A standard work on fruit and fruit-trees; the author having had over thirty years' practical experience at the head of one of the largest nurseries in this country. New edition, revised up to date. Invaluable to all fruit-growers. Illustrated. Cloth, 12mo. 2.00

The Propagation of Plants.

By Andrew S. Fuller. Illustrated with numerous engravings. An eminently practical and useful work. Describing the process of hybridizing and crossing species and varieties, and also the many different modes by which cultivated plants may be propagated and multiplied. Cloth, 12mo 1.50

Stewart's Shepherd's Manual.

A Valuable Practical Treatise on the Sheep for American farmers and sheep growers. It is so plain that a farmer, or a farmer's son, who has never kept a sheep. may learn from its pages how to manage a flock successfully, and yet so complete that even the experienced shepherd may gather many suggestions from it. The results of personal experience of some years with the characters of the various modern breeds of sheep, and the sheep-raising capabilities of many portions of our extensive territory and that of Canada—and the careful study of the diseases to which our sheep are chiefly subject, with those by which they may eventually be afflicted through unforeseen accidents—as well as the methods of management called for under our circumstances, are here gathered. By Henry Stewart. Illustrated. Cloth, 12mo.... 1.50

Allen's American Cattle.

Their History, Breeding, and Management. By Lewis F. Allen. This Book will be considered indispensable by every breeder of live stock. The large experience of the author in improving the character of American herds adds to the weight of his observations, and has enabled him to produce a work which will at once make good his claims as a standard authority on the subject. New and revised edition. Illustrated. Cloth, 12mo 2 50

Fuller's Grape Culturist.

By. A. S. Fuller. This is one of the very best of works on the culture of the hardy grapes, with full directions for all departments of propagation, culture, etc., with 150 excellent engravings, illustrating planting, training, grafting, etc. Cloth, 12mo 1.50

White's Cranberry Culture.

Contents:—Natural History.—History of Cultivation.—Choice of Location.—Preparing the Ground.—Planting the Vines.—Management of Meadows.—Flooding—Enemies and Difficulties Overcome.—Picking.—Keeping.—Profit and Loss.—Letters from Practical Growers.—Insects Injurious to the Cranberry. By Joseph J. White. A practical grower. Illustrated. Cloth, 12mo. New and revised edition. 1.25

Herbert's Hints to Horse-Keepers.

This is one of the best and most popular works on the Horse in this country. A Complete Manual for Horsemen, embracing: How to Breed a Horse; How to Buy a Horse; How to Break a Horse; How to Use a Horse; How to Feed a Horse; How to Physic a Horse (Allopathy or Homœpathy); How to Groom a Horse; How to Drive a Horse; How to Ride a Horse, etc. By the late Henry William Herbert (Frank Forester). Beautifully Illustrated. Cloth, 12mo... 1.75

Henderson's Practical Floriculture.

By Peter Henderson. A guide to the successful propagation and cultivation of florists' plants. The work is not one for florists and gardeners only, but the amateur's wants are constantly kept in mind, and we have a very complete treatise on the cultivation of flowers under glass, or in the open air, suited to those who grow flowers for pleasure as well as those who make them a matter of trade. The work is characterized by the same radical common sense that marked the author's "Gardening for Profit," and it holds a high place in the estimation of lovers of agriculture. Beautifully illustrated. New and enlarged edition. Cloth, 12mo 1.50

Harris's Talks on Manures.

By Joseph Harris, M. S., author of "Walks and Talks on the Farm," "Harris on the Pig." etc. Revised and enlarged by the author. A series of familiar and practical talks between the author and the deacon, the doctor, and other neighbors, on the whole subject of manures and fertilizers; including a chapter specially written for it by Sir John Bennet Lawes, of Rothamsted, England. Cloth, 12mo 1.75

Waring's Draining for Profit and Draining for Health.

This book is a very complete and practical treatise, the directions in which are plain, and easily followed. The subject of thorough farm drainage is discussed in all its bearings, and also that more extensive land drainage by which the sanitary condition of any district may be greatly improved, even to the banishment of fever and ague, typhoid and malarious fever. By Geo. E. Waring, Jr. Illustrated, Cloth 12mo. 1.50

The Practical Rabbit-Keeper.

By Cuniculus. Illustrated. A comprehensive work on keeping and raising Rabbits for pleasure as well as for profit. The book is abundantly illustrated with all the various Courts, Warrens, Hutches, Fencing, etc., and also with excellent portraits of the most important species of rabbits throughout the world. 12mo 1.50

Quinby's New Bee-Keeping.

The Mysteries of Bee-keeping Explained. Combining the results of Fifty Years' Experience, with the latest discoveries and inventions, and presenting the most approved methods, forming a complete work. Cloth, 12mo 1.50

Profits in Poultry.

Useful and Ornamental Breeds and their Profitable Management. This excellent work contains the combined experience of a number of practical men in all departments of poultry raising. It is profusely illustrated and forms an unique and important addition to our poultry literature. Cloth, 12mo 1.00

Barn Plans and Outbuildings.

Two Hundred and Fifty-seven Illustrations. A most Valuable Work, full of Ideas, Hints, Suggestions, Plans, etc., for the Construction of Barns and Outbuildings, by Practical writers. Chapters are devoted, among other subjects, to the Economic Erection and Use of Barns. Grain Barns, House Barns, Cattle Barns, Sheep Barns, Corn Houses, Smoke Houses, Ice Houses, Pig Pens, Granaries, etc. There are likewise chapters upon Bird Houses, Dog Houses, Tool Sheds, Ventilators, Roofs and Roofing, Doors and Fastenings, Work Shops, Poultry Houses, Manure Sheds, Barn Yards, Root Pits, etc. Recently published. Cloth, 12mo 1.50

Parsons on the Rose.

By Samuel B. Parsons. A treatise on the propagation, culture, and history of the rose. New and revised edition. In his work upon the rose, Mr. Parsons has gathered up the curious legends concerning the flower, and gives us an idea of the esteem in which it was held in former times. A simple garden classification has been adopted, and the leading varieties under each class enumerated and briefly described. The chapters on multiplication, cultivation, and training are very full, and the work is altogether one of the most complete before the public. Illustrated. Cloth, 12mo........................1.00

Heinrich's Window Flower Garden.

The author is a practical florist, and this enterprising volume embodies his personal experiences in Window Gardening during a long period. New and enlarged edition. By Julius J. Heinrich. Fully Illustrated. Cloth, 12mo.. .75

Liautard's Chart of the Age of the Domestic Animals.

Adopted by the United States Army. Enables one to accurately determine the age of horses, cattle, sheep, dogs, and pigs.......... .50

Pedder's Land Measurer for Farmers.

A convenient Pocket Companion, showing at once the contents of any piece of land, when its length and width are known, up to 1,500 feet either way, with various other useful farm tables. Cloth, 18mo; .60

How to Plant and What to Do with the Crops.

With other valuable hints for the Farm, Garden and Orchard. By Mark W. Johnson. Illustrated. CONTENTS: Times for Sowing Seeds: Covering Seeds; Field Crops; Garden or Vegetable Seeds, Sweet Herbs, etc.; Tree Seeds; Flower Seeds; Fruit Trees; Distances Apart for Fruit Trees and Shrubs; Profitable Farming; Green or Manuring Crops; Root Crops; Forage Plants; What to do with the Crops; The Rotation of Crops; Varieties; Paper Covers, post-paid.......... .50

Your Plants.

Plain and Practical Directions for the Treatment of Tender and Hardy Plants in the House and in the Garden. By James Sheehan. The above title well describes the character of the work—"Plain and Practical." The author, a commercial florist and gardener, has endeavored, in this work, to answer the many questions asked by his customers, as to the proper treatment of plants. The book shows all through that its author is a practical man, and he writes as one with a large store of experience. The work better meets the wants of the amateur who grows a few plants in the window, or has a small flower Garden, than a larger treatise intended for those who cultivate plants upon a more extended scale. Price, post-paid, paper covers................ .40

Husmann's American Grape-Growing and Wine-Making.

By George Husmann of Talcoa vineyards, Napa, California. New and enlarged edition. With contributions from well-known grape-growers, giving a wide range of experience. The author of this book is a recognized uthority on the subject. Cloth, 12mo............... 1.50

The Scientific Angler.

A general and instructive work on Artistic Angling, by the late David Foster. Complied by his Sons. With an Introductory Chapter and Copious Foot Notes, by William C. Harris, Editor of the "American Angler." Cloth, 12mo.. 1.50

Keeping One Cow.

A collection of Prize Essays, and selections from a number of other Essays, with editorial notes, suggestions, etc. This book gives the latest information, and in a clear and condensed form, upon the management of a single Milch Cow. Illustrated with full-page engravings of the most famous dairy cows. Recently published. Cloth, 12mo 1.00

Law's Veterinary Adviser

A Guide to the Prevention and Treatment of Disease in Domestic Animals. This is one of the best works on this subject, and is especially designed to supply the need of the busy American Farmer, who can rarely avail himself of the advice of a Scientific Veterinarian. It is brought up to date and treats of the Prevention of Disease, as well as of the Remedies. By Prof. Jas. Law. Cloth, Crown 8vo..... 3.00

Guenon's Treatise on Milch Cows.

A Treatise on the Bovine Species in General. An entirely new translation of the last edition of this popular and instructive book. By Thos. J. Hand, Secretary of the American Jersey Cattle Club. With over 100 Illustrations, especially engraved for this work. Cloth, 12mo. 1.00

The Cider Maker's Handbook.

A complete guide for making and keeping pure cider. By J. M. Trowbridge. Fully Illustrated. Cloth, 12mo........ 1.00

Long's Ornamental Gardening for Americans.

A treatise on Beautifying Homes, Rural Districts, and Cemeteries. A plain and practical work at a moderate price, with numerous illustrations, and instructions so plain that they may be readily followed. By Elias A. Long. Landscape Architect. Illustrated. Cloth, 12mo. 2.00

The Dogs of Great Britain, America and Other Countries.

New, enlarged and revised edition. Their breeding, training and management, in health and disease; comprising all the essential parts of the two standard works on the dog, by "Stonehenge," thereby furnishing for $2 what once cost $11.25. Contains Lists of all Premiums given at the last Dog Shows. It Describes the Best Game and Hunting Grounds in America. Contains over One Hundred Beautiful Engravings, embracing most noted Dogs in both Continents, making together, with Chapters by American Writers, the most Complete Dog Book ever published. Cloth, 12mo........ 2.00

Stewart's Feeding Animals.

By Elliot W. Stewart. A new and valuable practical work upon the laws of animal growth, specially applied to the rearing and feeding horses, cattle, diary cows, sheep and swine. Illustrated. Cloth, 12mo. 2.00

How to Co-operate.

A Manual for Co-operators. By Herbert Myrick. This book describes the how rather than the wherefore of co-operation. In other words it tells how to manage a co-operative store, farm or factory, and co-operative dairying, banking and fire insurance, and co-operative farmers' and women's exchanges for both buying and selling. The directions given are based on the actual experience of successful co-operative enterprises in all parts of the United States. The character and usefulness of the book commend it to the attention of all men and women who desire to better their condition. 12mo. Cloth........ 1.50

Batty's Practical Taxidermy and Home Decoration.
By Joseph H. Batty, taxidermist for the government surveys and many colleges and museums in the United States. An entirely new and complete as well as authentic work on taxidermy—giving in detail full directions for collecting and mounting animals, birds, reptiles, fish, insects, and general objects of natural history. 125 illustrations. Cloth, 12mo.. 1.50

Stewart's Irrigation for the Farm, Garden, and Orchard.
New and Enlarged Edition. This work is offered to those American Farmers, and other cultivators of the soil, who from painful experience can readily appreciate the losses which result from the scarcity of water at critical periods. By Henry Stewart. Fully illustrated. Cloth, 12mo.. 1.50

Johnson's How Crops Grow.
New Edition, entirely rewritten. A Treatise on the Chemical Composition, Structure, and Life of the Plant. Revised Edition. This book is a guide to the knowledge of agricultural plants, their composition, their structure, and modes of development and growth; of the complex organization of plants, and the use of the parts; the germination of seeds, and the food of plants obtained both from the air and the soil. The book is an invaluable one to all real students of agriculture. With numerous illustrations and tables of analysis. By Prof. Samuel W. Johnson, of Yale College. Cloth, 12mo............ 2.00

Johnson's How Crops Feed.
A treatise on the Atmosphere and the Soil, as related in the Nutrition of Agricultural Plants. The volume—the companion and complement to "How Crops Grow,"—has been welcomed by those who appreciate scientific aspects of agriculture. Illustrated. By Prof. Samuel W. Johnson. Cloth, 12mo.. 2.00

Warington's Chemistry of the Farm.
Treating with the utmost clearness and conciseness, and in the most popular manner possible, of the relations of Chemistry to Agriculture, and providing a welcome manual for those, who, while not having time to systematically study Chemistry, will gladly have such an idea as this gives them of its relation to operations on the farm. By R. Warington, F. C. S. Cloth, 12mo............................. 1.00

French's Farm Drainage.
The Principles, Process, and Effects of Draining Land, with Stones, Wood, Ditch-plows, Open Ditches, and especially with Ties; including Tables of Rainfall, Evaporation, Filteration, Excavation, Capacity of Pipes, cost and number to the acre. By Judge French, of New Hampshire. Cloth, 12mo...................................... 1.50

Hunter and Trapper.
The best modes of Hunting and Trapping are fully explained, and Foxes, Deer, Bears, etc., fall into his traps readily by following his directions. By Halsey Thrasher, an old and experienced sportsman. Cloth, 12mo.. .75

The American Merino. For Wool or for Mutton.
A practical and most valuable work on the selection, care, breeding and diseases of the Merino sheep, in all sections of the the United States. It is a full and exhaustive treatise upon this one breed of sheep. By Stephen Powers. Cloth, 12mo....................... 1.50

Armatage's Every Man His Own Horse Doctor.

By Prof. George Armatage, M. R. C. V. S. A valuable and comprehensive guide for both the professional and general reader with the fullest and latest information regarding all diseases, local injuries, lameness, operations, poisons, the dispensatory, etc., etc., with practical anatomical and surgical Illustrations. New Edition. Together with Blaine's "Veterinary Art," and numerous recipes. One large 8vo. volume, 830 pages, half morocco.......... 7.50

Dadd's Modern Horse Doctor.

Containing Practical Observations on the Causes, Nature, and Treatment of Diseases and Lameness of Horses—embracing recent and improved Methods, according to an enlightened system of Veterinary Practice, for Preservation and Restoration of Health. Illustrated. By Geo. H. Dadd, M. D. V. S., Cloth, 12mo.......... 1.50

The Family Horse.

Its Stabling, Care, and Feeding. By Geo. A. Martin. A Practical Manual, full of the most useful information. Illustrated. Cloth, 12mo.......... 1.00

Sander's Horse Breeding.

Being the general principles of Heredity applied to the Business of Breeding Horses and the Management of Stallions, Brood Mares and Foals. The book embraces all that the breeder should know in regard to the selection of stock, management of the stallion, brood mare, and foal, and treatment of diseases peculiar to breeding animals. By J. H. Sanders. 12mo, cloth.......... 2.00

Coburn's Swine Husbandry.

New, revised and enlarged edition. The Breeding, Rearing and Management of Swine, and the Prevention and Treatment of their Diseases. It is the fullest and freshest compendium relating to Swine Breeding yet offered. By F. D. Coburn. Cloth, 12mo.......... 1.75

Dadd's American Cattle Doctor.

By George H. Dadd, M. D., Veterinary Practitioner. To help every man to be his own cattle-doctor; giving the necessary information for preserving the health and curing the diseases of oxen, cows, sheep, and swine, with a great variety of original recipes, and valuable information on farm and dairy management. Cloth, 12mo.......... 1.50

Silos, Ensilage, and Silage.

A practical treatise on the Ensilage of Fodder Corn. Containing the most recent and authentic information on this important subject, by Manly Miles, M.D., F.R.M.S. Illustrated. Cloth 12mo.......... .50

Broom Corn and Brooms.

A Treatise on Raising Broom-Corn and Making Brooms on a small or Large Scale. Illustrated. 12mo. Cloth cover.......... .50

American Bird Fancier.

Or how to breed, rear, and care for Song and Domestic Birds. This valuable and important little work for all who are interested in the keeping of Song Birds, has been revised and enlarged, and is now a complete manual upon the subject. All who own valuable birds, or wish to do so, will find the new Fancier indispensable. New, revised and enlarged edition. By D. J. Browne, and Dr. Fuller Walker. Illustrated, paper cover.......... .50

www.ingramcontent.com/pod-product-compliance
Lightning Source LLC
Chambersburg PA
CBHW020850270326
41928CB00006B/628
9783337287504